C I T Y P A C K
San Francisco

By Mick Sinclair

W/p.

Fodor's

Fodor's Travel Publications, Inc.

New York

Page 1: Baker Beach

Page 2 (above): Alamo Square Park

Page 5 (a): North Beach
Page 5 (b): Carnival time

Page 13 (a): Carnival time
Page 13 (b): Chinatown

Page 23 (a): The Modern Art Gallery
Page 23 (b): Chinatown

Page 49 (a): Fisherman's Wharf
Page 49 (b): Columbus Tower

Page 61 (a): Mural in Fulton Street
Page 61 (b): Barman in The Haight

Page 87 (a): Maritime Museum
Page 87 (b): Cable car

© 1996 by The Automobile Association
Maps copyright 1996 © by The Automobile Association
Fold-out map:
        © RV Reise- und Verkehrsverlag Munich . Stuttgart
        © Cartography: GeoData

Published in the United States by Fodor's Travel Publications, Inc.
Published in the United Kingdom by AA Publishing

Fodor's is a trademark of Fodor's Travel Publications, Inc.

ISBN 0-679-02962-1
First Edition

Fodor's Citypack San Francisco
Author: Mick Sinclair
Cartography: The Automobile Association
                RV Reise- und Verkehrsverlag
Cover Design: Tigist Getachew, Fabrizio La Rocca

Special Sales

Origination by BTB Colour Reproduction Ltd, Whitchurch, Hampshire.
Manufactured by Dai Nippon Printing Co. (Hong Kong) Ltd.

10 9 8 7 6 5 4 3 2 1

Contents

About this book

Citypack San Francisco is divided into six sections to cover the six most important aspects of your visit to San Francisco.

1 SAN FRANCISCO LIFE
(pages 5–12)
Your personal introduction to San Francisco by author Mick Sinclair
Facts and figures
Leading characters
Big events in San Francisco's history

2 HOW TO ORGANIZE YOUR TIME *(pages 13–22)*
Make the most of your time in San Francisco
4 one-day itineraries
2 suggested walks
4 evening strolls
Organized sightseeing
4 excursions beyond the city
Calendar of events

3 SAN FRANCISCO'S TOP 25 SIGHTS *(pages 23–48)*
Mick Sinclair's own choice, including his personal introduction to each sight
Description and history
Highlights of each attraction
Comprehensive practical information
Each sight located on the inside cover of the book

4 SAN FRANCISCO'S BEST
(pages 49–60)
What San Francisco is renowned for
Neighborhoods, Places of Worship, Museums, Buildings, Parks, Attractions and Streets
Practical details throughout

5 SAN FRANCISCO: WHERE TO... *(pages 61–86)*
The best places to eat, shop, be entertained and stay
10 categories of restaurants
8 categories of stores
6 categories of entertainment spots
3 categories of hotels
Price bands and booking details

6 SAN FRANCISCO TRAVEL FACTS *(pages 87–93)*
Essential information for your stay

SYMBOLS
Throughout the guide a few straightforward symbols are used to denote the following categories:

✚	map reference on the foldout map accompanying this book (see below)
⊠	address
☎	telephone number
◉	opening times
❙❙	restaurant or café on premises or near by
⊖	nearest subway station
⊟	nearest bus/trolleybus/trolley route
⊞	nearest overground train station
⅃	facilities for visitors with disabilities
⊞	admission charge
↔	other places of interest nearby
?	tours, lectures, or special events
➤	indicates the page where you will find a fuller description

MAPS
All map references are to the separate foldout map accompanying this book. For example, the Asian Art Museum in Golden Gate Park has the following information ✚ E7 – indicating the grid square in which the Asian Art Museum will be found.

All entries within the Top 25 Sights section are also plotted by number (not page number) on the downtown plan located on the inside front and back covers of this book.

PRICES
Where appropriate, the cost of an establishment is indicated by $ signs: $$$ denotes higher prices; $$ denotes average prices; $ denotes lower charges.

SAN FRANCISCO *life*

917.9

148760

A Personal View

Carnival in the Mission District

The "F" word

The worst mistake a newcomer to San Francisco is likely to make is not stumbling into a threatening neighborhood but calling the city "Frisco," a term known locally as the "F word." Visitors can, however, earn themselves considerable respect by adopting the habit, which extends across all of northern California, of referring to San Francisco simply as "the city."

Since the 1850s Gold Rush transformed it almost overnight from a hamlet into a city, San Francisco has been different from the rest. The anything-goes atmosphere of the early days has helped create a city that thrives on tolerance and change. San Francisco has frequently set the nation's cultural and social pace—witnessing the birth of 1950s Beats, of 1960s hippies, of 1970s gay and lesbian liberation—and is currently vibrant with media and software companies alert to the possibilities of the global information revolution; computer-dominated "Silicon Valley" is just an hour's drive away. As California approaches the 21st century, the state is set to become the first in the United States without an ethnic majority. San Francisco, home to a multitude of races, religions and cultures, is a symbol of this multiculturalism.

Besides its intense cosmopolitanism, San Francisco is also full of quickly revealed idiosyncrasies. Cable cars, steep streets, morning fogs, and intricate Victorian architecture are all part of San Francisco's character and help fuel the pride that the majority of its residents feel, as does the proliferation of cafés, where smoking may be frowned upon but coffee is regarded as the elixir of life.

With 18 million annual arrivals, San Francisco is the most visited city in the United States and tourism has been its major source of income since the 1970s. As a result, the city is noticeably visitor-friendly, with information easily accessed and opportunities to explore beneath the surface—such as the guided walking tours that gleefully lift the lid on the city—being plentiful.

Geography has done San Francisco many favors, most obviously in enabling the city to occupy a peninsula that is scenically spectacular and that prevents the onset of urban sprawl. Instead, the city is compact and divides into a network of neighborhoods, all of them linked by public transportation.

Geology has been less benevolent, with several major fault lines close to the city. An earthquake destroyed San Francisco completely in 1906, another inflicted major damage in 1989, and a major quake might strike at any time. Visitors might take solace in the statistical unlikelihood of this occurring during their stay and the fact that San Francisco is among the world leaders in earthquake preparedness: basic precautions are even suggested in the city phone book.

Buses

San Francisco is easy to travel around by bus, but actual bus numbers can be confusing. Throughout this book, we indicate the numbered bus routes passing by or close to a particular site, though the city's one-way system causes buses to follow slightly different outbound and inbound routes.

A mural in the Mission District illustrates the multicultural nature of San Francisco's population

SAN FRANCISCO IN FIGURES

DISTANCES	Distance from New York: 2,930 miles Distance from Los Angeles: 397 miles Distance from London: 6,010 miles Distance from Berlin: 6,094 miles
SIZE	Population: 724,000, 14th largest city in USA Area: 46.38 square miles Miles of waterfront: 7.5 Miles of shoreline: 8.4
GEOGRAPHY	Latitude: N 37° 46' 39" Longitude: W 122° 24'40" Foundation: sandstone, shale, volcanic rock Highest point: Mt Davidson, 938 feet Lowest point: sea level Hills: 43 Islands within city limits: 11 Park acreage within city limits: 8,100
HISTORY	Founded: Presidio of San Francisco, September 17, 1776 Oldest structure: Mission Dolores 1791 Population at first census, 1798: 627
STREETS OF SAN FRANCISCO	Longest street: Mission Street Widest street: Van Ness Avenue Steepest streets: Filbert between Leavenworth and Hyde, and 22nd Street between Church and Vicksburg, both with 31.5 percent gradients
SYMBOLS	City flag: a Phoenix rising from the ashes on a white background bordered by gold Official flower: dahlia Official song: *San Francisco* Official ballad: *I Left My Heart in San Francisco* Official motto: *Oro en paz, Fierro en guerra* ("Gold in peace, Iron in war")
WEATHER	Wettest month: January, 4.48 inches Driest month: July, 0.04 inches Warmest month: September, mean maximum 68.9°F Coolest month: January, mean maximum 56.1°F Annual mean temperatures: high 62.5°F; low 51°F

SAN FRANCISCO PEOPLE

HERB CAEN

Herb Caen's by-line first appeared in the *San Francisco Chronicle* in the 1930s, since when he became, and remains, the city's most widely read columnist. Be it city politics or the latest in-vogue restaurant, Caen's love of San Francisco and awareness of its traditions always shines through.

FRANCIS FORD COPPOLA

Detroit-born Francis Ford Coppóla rose to prominence as director of *The Godfather*. He located his independent Zoetrope film company in San Francisco during the 1970s. Coppola's money saved the flatiron-style Columbus Tower from demolition. He is frequently to be seen in and around North Beach restaurants.

Francis Ford Coppola

DIANNE FEINSTEIN

Feinstein became city mayor through the assassination of the incumbent in 1978 and defied expectations by winning the two subsequent mayoral elections. Having raised the profile of women in city politics and given a platform to sexual minority groups, Feinstein was elected to represent California in the U.S. Senate.

LAWRENCE FERLINGHETTI

Ferlinghetti's poetry helped to make him one of the leading figures of the 1950s Beat Generation, as did his co-ownership of the City Lights bookstore, the country's first exclusively paperback bookshop, which published, to great controversy, Allen Ginsberg's seminal *Howl* in 1956.

DAVID SMITH

As an idealistic medical student, Smith founded the Haight-Ashbury Free Clinic during 1967 when San Francisco's hippie population was poorly served by established medical facilities. Smith's free clinics grew in number and now operate from 20 sites around the Bay Area, serving an average of 800 low-income patients a day.

The Grateful Dead

Formed in the mid-1960s to play LSD-influenced R&B music for hours at a time to the residents of Haight-Ashbury, the Grateful Dead were among the original psychedelic rock bands that helped to make San Francisco the heart of the hippie movement. They continued to be enormously popular for three decades, still cherishing their original idealistic beliefs, but the death in 1995 of lead guitarist Jerry Garcia drew to an end this chapter in San Francisco's musical life.

A CHRONOLOGY

Pre-1776	An estimated 13,000 Native Americans live on either side of the Golden Gate.
1776	Traveling from their Californian base at Monterey, the Spanish build a *presidio* (or garrison) and mission on the northern tip of the San Francisco peninsula.
1821	Newly independent Mexico acquires California from Spain.
1846	USA takes control of California.
1848	Gold discovered near Sacramento, 87 miles northeast of San Francisco.
1849	The California Gold Rush begins. San Francisco's population soars from 812 to 20,000.
1851	San Francisco becomes the fourth-busiest port in the United States.
1853	An ill-fated attempt to corner the rice market leads to the bankruptcy of entrepreneur Joshua Norton, who assumes a new identity as Emperor Norton and becomes a celebrated eccentric (▶12).
1873	The city's first cable car runs along Clay Street.
1906	On April 18 a major earthquake (8.3 on the Richter Scale) followed by a three-day fire leaves 3,700 dead and destroys 28,000 buildings.
1915	The Panama Pacific Exposition symbolizes the city's recovery from the earthquake.
1934	Police fatally shoot two striking dockers and 150,000 people join a four-day general strike in protest.
1936	Bay Bridge completed.
1937	Golden Gate Bridge completed.
1941	U.S. entry into World War II stimulates war

industries and brings an influx of military and civilian personnel to San Francisco. Employment in the city's shipyards grows from 4,000 to 260,000.

1945
The United Nations charter is signed by 50 countries in the San Francisco Opera House; the Soviet Union vetoes a proposal to make San Francisco the UN's permanent home.

1957
Publication of Allen Ginsberg's poem *Howl* by North Beach bookstore-publisher City Lights helps the neighborhood become the centre of an influx of what *San Francisco Chronicle* columnist Herb Caen labels "beatniks."

1964
Students at Berkeley form the nonviolent Free Speech Movement and instigate the first of the campus revolts that spread across the country in succeeding years.

1966
Militant African-American group, the Black Panthers, forms in Oakland.

1967
As young people arrive from all across the country during what is later termed the "Summer of Love," Haight-Ashbury's hippie population grows from 7,000 to 75,000.

1977
Harvey Milk becomes the nation's first openly gay candidate to be elected to public office.

1978
Harvey Milk and Mayor George Moscone assassinated at City Hall by a former city politician, Dan White.

1979
The lightweight five-year prison sentence bestowed on White prompts the "White Night Riot" when predominantly gay demonstrators march on City Hall, causing $1 million worth of damage.

1989
The Loma Prieta earthquake (7.1 on the Richter Scale) kills 67 people and closes the Bay Bridge for a month.

1991
Fires rage across the Oakland Hills on the east side of San Francisco Bay, killing 25 and destroying 3,000 homes.

11

PEOPLE & EVENTS FROM HISTORY

The Big Four

The so-called Big Four—Charles Crocker, Mark Hopkins, Collis P. Huntington, and Leland Stanford—were Gold-Rush shopkeepers who joined forces in 1865 to form the Southern Pacific Railroad. This was the first transcontinental railroad and the enterprise not only earned fortunes for the Big Four but also fueled a corrupt business empire that dominated San Franciscan life for decades.

The 1906 earthquake and fire

The earthquake that struck at 5:12A.M. on April 18, 1906, a product of the San Andreas Fault, caused relatively minor damage in itself but by rupturing gas and water mains it enabled fires to break out and burn uncontrolled. The fires eventually left 3,000 acres of San Francisco devastated and rendered 250,000 of the city's 400,000 inhabitants homeless.

EMPEROR NORTON

Wearing epaulettes and a cockaded hat, former businessman Joshua Norton proclaimed himself "Emperor of the United States and Protector of Mexico" in 1856. He spent the rest of his life wandering San Francisco's streets, issuing proclamations and collecting a 50¢-a-month levy for his "court expenses." On his death in 1880, flags flew at half-mast and his funeral was attended by the mayor.

LILLIE COIT

Raised for high society, Lillie Coit outraged her peers by wearing men's clothes, playing poker with dockers, smoking cigars and taking a special interest in San Francisco's volunteer fire brigades. When she died in 1929, Lillie left $100,000 for the beautification of the city, and it was decided to use these funds to erect a memorial—the present Coit Tower—to the city's volunteer firefighters.

JOHN MCLAREN

Born in Scotland in 1846, John McLaren migrated to California and became supervisor of Golden Gate Park. So well-known did the "tyrannical and capricious" Scot become in San Francisco that his birthday was celebrated as a civic event, and a special law was passed in 1917 enabling him to work beyond retirement age. McLaren continued as park supervisor until his death in 1943.

Coit Tower, erected as a memorial to Lillie Coit

SAN FRANCISCO
how to organize your time

ITINERARIES

Steep hills notwithstanding, San Francisco is well suited to walking and has an excellent public transportation system. If your time is limited, careful planning will ensure that you get the most from this fascinating city and its environs.

ITINERARY ONE	ALCATRAZ TO TELEGRAPH HILL
Morning	Avoid tourist crowds by taking the first ferry from Fisherman's Wharf to Alcatraz (➤ 38).
	Returning from Alcatraz, walk or take public transportation from Fisherman's Wharf to North Beach (➤ 51). Explore North Beach's cafés and bookshops, the North Beach Museum (➤ 53), Washington Square (➤ 56) and the Church of Saints Peter and Paul (➤ 52).
Lunch	Mario's Bohemian Cigar Store or Caffè Trieste (➤ 68); North Beach Pizza (➤ 63), Basta Pasta (➤ 65), or Fior d'Italia (➤ 65).
Afternoon	Continue to Telegraph Hill's Coit Tower (➤ 57) and the flower-lined Filbert Steps (➤ 60).
ITINERARY TWO	CHINATOWN TO FORT MASON CENTER
Morning	Stroll through Chinatown (➤ 50), visiting the three temples of Waverly Place (➤ 60) and the neighborhood shops (➤ 76).
Lunch	Sample a Chinatown *dim sum* lunch at Pot Sticker or Royal Jade (➤ 64), which also has a buffet, or try the House of Nanking (➤ 64).
Afternoon	Walk or take public transportation to Russian Hill (➤ 51), visiting Ina Coolbrith Park (➤ 56), and stroll along Green Street (➤ 60).
	Continue to Pacific Heights (➤ 51), walk through Lafayette Park (➤ 56), then explore the shops and restaurants of Union Street (➤ 60).
	Take public transportation to Fort Mason Center (➤ 35) and explore the museums.

ITINERARY THREE	NOB HILL TO SOMA

Morning
Start the day at Nob Hill (➤ 50).
Tour Grace Cathedral (➤ 40) and look inside some of the neighborhood's exclusive hotels. Walk or take public transportation to the Financial District. Visit the distinctive Transamerica Pyramid (➤ 45), view the 19th-century buildings of Jackson Square and the towering Bank of America HQ (➤ 54). Tour the Wells Fargo Museum (➤ 46) inside the Wells Fargo Bank.

Lunch
Financial District luxury options are Aqua and Tommy Toy's (➤ 62); less expensive options are Yank Sing (➤ 64) and Café Bastille (➤ 68).

Afternoon
Take public transportation to SoMa (➤ 51) and spend the rest of the day at the San Francisco Museum of Modern Art (➤ 44).

Refreshment
The Compass Rose (➤ 69).

ITINERARY FOUR	HAIGHT-ASHBURY TO GOLDEN GATE PARK

Morning
Start the day in Haight-Ashbury (➤ 50).
Tour some of the neighborhood's streets, lined by Victorian homes and landmarks from 1960s hippiedom. Browse Haight Street's unusual shops.

Lunch
Haight-Ashbury's Kan Zaman or Jammin' Java (➤ 68).

Afternoon
Walk from Haight-Ashbury into Golden Gate Park (➤ 25). Visit the park's Conservatory of Flowers and continue to the M. H. De Young Memorial Museum (➤ 29) and Asian Art Museum (➤ 28). With children, allocate time for the park's California Academy of Sciences (➤ 30).
Should the park be of more appeal than its museums, rent a bicycle from one of the outlets along Stanyan Street and tour its full extent.

Refreshment
The café at the M. H. De Young Memorial Museum (➤ 29).

WALKS

One of the many skyscrapers of the Financial District

UNION SQUARE TO NORTH BEACH

Begin in the lobby of the Westin St. Francis Hotel(► 84), where the grandfather clock has long been a renowned San Franciscan meeting place. Leave the hotel and cross Union Square. Note the square's Dewey Monument, with its bronze figure of Victory reputedly modeled on Alma Spreckels (► 26).

Maiden Lane and the Financial District Leave the square, crossing Stockton Street for Maiden Lane (► 60). On Maiden Lane, note the Circle Gallery. From Maiden Lane, walk north along Kearny Street passing the Bank of America HQ, and turn left onto California Street, walking uphill and crossing the street for Old St. Mary's Church.

Coffee breaks Recommended stops for coffee are Franciscan Croissant, 301 Sutter Street on the corner with Grant Avenue (☎ 415/398 8276), with excellent coffee and extensive croissants and pastries; or Mocca on Maiden Lane, 175 Maiden Lane (☎ 415/956 1188), which has outdoor seating and hot, filling sandwiches.

Chinatown Stroll along Grant Avenue into the heart of Chinatown. Turn onto Commercial Street and visit the Chinese Historical Society of America. Afterward return to Grant Avenue and continue on to Waverly Place (► 60) and the Tien Hou Temple. Turn right along Washington Street to Portsmouth Square, noting the memorial on the north side to Robert Louis Stevenson, and go straight on for a visit to the Transamerica Pyramid.

Time for lunch Walk, or take a bus, along Columbus Avenue for North Beach and lunch. For lunch suggestions ► 14 (Itinerary One).

THE SIGHTS

- Circle Gallery (► 54)
- Bank of America HQ (► 54)
- Old St. Mary's Church (► 52)
- Chinese Historical Society of America (► 43)
- Tien Hou Temple (► 52)
- Transamerica Pyramid (► 45)

INFORMATION

Distance approx 1½ miles
Time 2 hours
Start point Westin St. Francis Hotel, Union Square
✚ K5
▣ 2, 3, 4, 6, 38, 71; Powell—Hyde and Powell—Mason cable cars
End point North Beach
✚ K3/4

WALKS

NORTH BEACH TO THE TRANSAMERICA PYRAMID

After lunch, browse around City Lights, a bookstore pivotal to the 1950s Beat Generation. Alongside, Jack Kerouac Street was named for one of the movement's leading figures, and the adjacent Vesuvio's (➤ 82) was a popular hangout. Across Columbus Avenue, note the Condor Bistro, formerly the Condor Club and, in 1964, scene of the first topless act in the United States (commemorated by a plaque).

North Beach museums and churches Cross to Stockton Street for the North Beach Museum. Return along Vallejo Street to Columbus Avenue, crossing the latter for the Church of St. Francis of Assisi, founded in 1849 and the first Catholic church in California since the Spanish missions. Continue north, browsing around Grant Avenue's unusual shops. Turn onto Union Street for Washington Square and the Church of Saints Peter and Paul. Climb Filbert Street (or use bus 39) to reach Coit Tower, then descend the Filbert Steps. In Montgomery Street, note the art deco apartment building at number 1360, which was featured, with Humphrey Bogart and Lauren Bacall, in the 1947 film *Dark Passage*. Follow Montgomery Street south to return to North Beach.

THE SIGHTS

- City Lights bookstore (➤ 73)
- North Beach Museum (➤ 53)
- Washington Square (➤ 56)
- Church of Saints Peter and Paul (➤ 52)
- Coit Tower (➤ 57)
- Filbert Steps (➤ 60)

INFORMATION

Distance 1¼ miles
Time 1½–2 hours
Start point City Lights bookstore
⊞ K4
🚌 15, 41, 83
End point Montgomery Street
⊞ L4

More Beat landmarks

Devotees of the 1950s Beat Generation might like to extend their walk to include 1010 Montgomery Street, Allen Ginsberg's home when he completed *Howl*. Ginsberg read the poem in public for the first time at 3119 Filmore Street, in Pacific Heights. Jack Kerouac, meanwhile, wrote parts of *On The Road* in the loft of 29 Russell Street, in Russian Hill.

Vesuvio's Coffee Bar, North Beach

EVENING STROLLS

San Francisco offers you a number of alluring possibilities for enjoying a pre-dinner tipple in interesting surroundings before taking a short, appetite-sharpening stroll to a restaurant.

The view from the Carnelian Room, Bank of America HQ

THE CARNELIAN ROOM & NORTH BEACH OR CHINATOWN

Start the evening with a drink at the Carnelian Room (►81), enjoying the view from this 52nd floor of the Bank of America HQ (►54). Afterwards, walk north into Chinatown or North Beach for dinner.

COIT TOWER & NORTH BEACH OR CHINATOWN

Take the bus or climb the hill leading to Coit Tower (►57; open until 7:30P.M. in summer, otherwise closing at 6) for a view across the city at twilight. Walk down the hill for dinner in North Beach or Chinatown.

THE FOUR SEASONS CLIFT HOTEL & UNION SQUARE

Relax with a cocktail amid the artworks in the Redwood Room of the Four Seasons Clift Hotel (►81) before strolling into the Union Square area for dinner.

THE MARRIOTT & SOMA OR UNION SQUARE

Escape the sight of what many San Franciscans consider a blight on the skyline by stepping inside the Marriott Hotel (►54) for a drink at the 39th-floor View Lounge. Afterwards, walk into SoMa or the Union Square area for dinner.

ORGANIZED SIGHTSEEING

WALKING TOURS

City Guides (☎ 415/557 4266) Operate free daily tours, including City Hall, Victorian era Haight-Ashbury, Nob Hill, Sutro Heights Park, the mansions of Pacific Heights, and the murals of the Mission District.

The Wok Wiz (☎ 415/355 9657) Popular tours that offer a three-hour introduction to Chinatown, visiting herb shops, artists, and historic sites, with an optional lunch that unravels the mysteries of *dim sum*.

Cruisin' the Castro (☎ 415/550 8110) Tours giving an excellent two-hour outline of San Francisco's gay and lesbian past take place in the Castro district.

Helen's Walk Tour (☎ 510/524 4544) Gives participants a choice of themes and areas, but is memorable above all for the infectious enthusiasm of the guide herself.

BOAT RIDES

Red & White Fleet (☎ 800/229 2784) Operate a 45-minute narrated cruise on San Francisco Bay, circling Alcatraz and Angel Island and passing beneath the Golden Gate Bridge.

Blue & Gold Fleet (☎ 415/705 5444) Offer a similar narrated bay voyage, but one that lasts 75 minutes and passes under the Bay Bridge as well as the Golden Gate Bridge.

BUS TOURS

If your time is very limited, a guided bus tour is one way to see the city highlights quickly. **Tower Tours** (☎ 415/434 TOUR) have a half-day tour of the city, which can be combined with a cruise on the bay.

Gray Line Tours (☎ 415/558 9400) offer a half-day tour and an evening tour that includes a walk around Chinatown and optional dinner.

Air Tours

For an overview of the city, San Francisco Helicopter Tours (☎ 800/400 2404) offer half-hour flights revealing the natural drama of the city and of San Francisco Bay from above. Prices start at $70.

On the evening ferry to Sausalito

19

EXCURSIONS

INFORMATION

Berkeley and Oakland

☎ For BART information
415/788 BART; Berkeley
Campus information
510/642 INFO; Oakland
Convention & Visitors
Bureau 510/839 9000;
Oakland–San Francisco
ferry Blue & Gold Fleet
510/552 3300.

🚇 For Berkeley use the
"Berkeley" stop; for
Oakland use "Lake Merritt"
for the museum and "12th
Street" for Chinatown

Sausalito and Tiburon

☎ Golden Gate Ferries
415/332 6600; Red &
White Fleet 800/229 2784

*The waterfront at
Sausalito*

BERKELEY & OAKLAND

Take BART to Berkeley. Walk to Berkeley
campus (►48) and explore its museums and
public buildings. From the campus, cross onto
Telegraph Avenue for lively restaurants and
bookstores. Continue by BART to Oakland.
Tour The Oakland Museum (►47). Walk north
from the museum to look across Lake Merritt.
Tour the 19th-century Camron Stanford House,
beside the lake. Take BART or bus to Oakland's
Chinatown and the shops and attractions of Jack
London Square. Return to San Francisco by
ferry for a dramatic view of the city's skyline.

SAUSALITO & TIBURON

Take a ferry from the Ferry Building or from
Fisherman's Wharf to Sausalito and explore its
downtown. Climb one of the hillside lanes for a
view across the bay to San Francisco. Walk
along Bridgeway to see waterside homes and
houseboats. Continue on foot, or take the bus,
along Bridgeway for the Bay Model, a large,
detailed scale model of San Francisco Bay's
waterways.

Continue by ferry from Sausalito to Tiburon.
Explore the shops and galleries in the wood-
framed buildings and the converted houseboats
of Ark Row. In summer, take the ferry from
Tiburon to Angel Island State Park and explore
the many bicycle and foot trails.

EXCURSIONS

THE NORTHERN COAST

Drive across the Golden Gate Bridge and head north on Highway 1, passing Muir Beach and Stinson Beach for the Audubon Canyon Ranch, where foot trails are open for birdwatchers from mid-March to July. Continue north around Bolinas Lagoon, reaching the village of Bolinas and the tidepools of Duxbury Point. Go on to Point Reyes National Seashore, land shaped by the geological upheavals of the San Andreas Fault. Returning south, take the Panoramic Highway into Mount Tamalpais State Park. Continue to the summit of Mount Tamalpais for a view across the bay toward the city.

INFORMATION

Audubon Canyon Ranch
   ☎ 414/868 9244
Point Reyes National Seashore
   Ranger Station
   ☎ 415/663 1092
Buena Vista Winery
   ☎ 707/938 1266
Jack London State Historic Park
   ☎ 707/938 5216
Château St. Jean
   ☎ 707/833 4134;
Petaluma's Adobe State Historic
   Park ☎ 707/762 4871

Sonoma Wine and Visitors Center holds extensive information on the many wineries of Sonoma County

SONOMA VALLEY

Drive across the Golden Gate Bridge and continue north on Highway 101, passing through San Rafael for the town of Sonoma. Explore the Sonoma Mission and the other restored historic buildings and shops around Sonoma Plaza. Continue to the Buena Vista Winery. Continue north to the hamlet of Glen Ellen and tour Jack London State Historic Park, former home of the writer whose name it bears. Continue north for Kenwood and a selection of wineries, such as Château St. Jean. Return to Sonoma and turn west along Highway 116 for Petaluma's Adobe State Historic Park.

Major car rental companies

Avis   ☎ 800/331 1212
Budget ☎ 800/527 0700
Dollar ☎ 800/800 4000
Hertz ☎ 800/654 3131

21

What's On

Barely a week goes by without a festival of some kind being celebrated in San Francisco. The Visitor Information Center, on the lower level of Hallidie Plaza, junction of Market and Powell streets (Mon–Fri 9–5:30, Sat 9–3, Sun 10–2; ☎415/391 2000), has an Events Hotline: ☎415/391 2001 (English); ☎415/391 2004 (German). The *San Francisco Bay Guardian* and *SF Weekly*, and the Datebook section of the Sunday *San Francisco Chronicle* and *San Francisco Examiner* all carry details of imminent happenings. The following are selected highlights.

JANUARY/ FEBRUARY	Chinese New Year: Two weeks of Chinatown festivities; date depends on the lunar cycle.
MARCH	St. Patrick's Day (Mar 17): Irish and would-be-Irish San Franciscans dress in green for a parade along Market Street.
APRIL	Cherry Blossom Festival: A celebration of Japanese art and culture in Japantown.
MAY	*Cinco de Mayo* (May 5): Mexican celebration centered in Mission District. Bay to Breakers: Athletes and exhibitionists race from one side of the city to the other. Carnival: Mission District fills with music, floats, and colorful costumes.
JUNE	Lesbian & Gay Freedom Day: Huge gay and lesbian march that winds from the Castro district to Civic Center Plaza.
JULY	Independence Day (July 4): The national celebration is marked by fireworks and a 50-cannon salute on the northern waterfront. San Francisco Marathon: The country's third-largest marathon includes a crossing of the Golden Gate Bridge.
SEPTEMBER	San Francisco Blues Festival (last weekend Sep) ➤79.
OCTOBER	Halloween Parade (Oct 31): Outrageous costumes are shown off along Castro Street.
NOVEMBER	Day of the Dead (Nov 2): Mexican tribute to the spirit world includes a macabre art exhibition and a parade through the Mission District.

SAN FRANCISCO's
top 25 sights

The sights are numbered from west to east across the city

GOLDEN GATE NRA

An enormous swath of mostly un-developed land lying within the city and extending northward across the Golden Gate Bridge, the Golden Gate National Recreation Area is to me a wonderful reminder of how open and wild most of California is.

HIGHLIGHTS

- Coastal trail
- China Beach
- Baker Beach
- Fort Point
- Seal Rocks
- Fort Funston
- Marin Headlands
- Point Bonita Lighthouse
- Ocean Beach
- Golden Gate Promenade

INFORMATION

- ➕ A/B/C/D/E/F/G/H/J 1/3/4/5/6/7/8/9/10 and off map
- ✉ GGNRA Headquarters: Building 201, Fort Mason Center
- ☎ Cliff House Visitor Center (➕ A6) 415/556 8642
- 🕐 Daylight hours only recommended; Visitor Center daily 10–4:30
- 🚌 5, 18, 19, 28, 29, 30, 31, 32, 38, 42, 48, 76
- ♿ None to excellent according to location; for details ☎ 415/556 0560
- 🎟 Free
- ↔ Fort Mason Center (➤ 35), Golden Gate Bridge (➤ 27), Marina Green (➤ 56), National Maritime Museum (➤ 53), San Francisco Zoo (➤ 58), Sutro Heights Park (➤ 57).
- ❓ Ranger-led tours

Creation From the cliffs of Fort Funston in the south to the hills of Marin County in the north, the Golden Gate National Recreation Area (GGNRA) bestows federal protection on a long, slender chunk of San Francisco's coastline. GGNRA's 74,000 acres, which lie in separate pockets and often lack clearly marked boundaries, were created in 1972 by the amalgamation of city parks, private land, and former military-owned areas. GGNRA's abandoned fortifications include a Civil War fort (Fort Point, located beneath the Golden Gate Bridge) and a massive World War II cannon at Baker Beach.

Exploration Much of GGNRA is best explored on foot. Start at the Cliff House Visitor Center, close to the sea lion-frequented Seal Rocks, and walk the blustery coastal trail that weaves through the coarsely vegetated hillsides that rise steeply above the tiny beach of Lands End and the forbidding waters of the Golden Gate. All vestiges of the city are entirely hidden until the appearance of the Golden Gate Bridge. This route also brings views of the isolated China Beach, named for the Chinese fishermen of the Gold Rush-era who lived in shacks beside it. China Beach is one of the few San Francisco beaches that is safe for swimming. The more accessible Baker Beach, however, although swimming is not permitted, is the perfect spot for a rest.

GOLDEN GATE PARK

To my mind, Golden Gate Park is not only a massive slab of greenery holding several oustanding museums but it also provides a stage for San Francisco—and its jogging, kite-flying, roller-skating population—to present itself to the outside world.

Acres of fun Three miles long and half-a-mile wide, Golden Gate Park is one of the world's largest urban parks. Secreted within its 1,000 acres are a polo field, a golf course, an archery range, a botanical garden, two major museums and the California Academy of Sciences, countless lakes, ponds, and waterfalls and even a couple of windmills. Yet there is still sufficient space to become hopelessly lost—and quickly found again—around its tree-shrouded lanes and footpaths.

On foot The park is too large to cover entirely on foot but the eastern half edge is fine for strolling. Here you will find the redstone McLaren Lodge, former office of the park's creator and now an information center (maps are essential), and the 1878 Conservatory, with palm trees, water lilies, and orchids flourishing in its humid interior. Also within easy reach is the Japanese Tea Garden, with azaleas, cherry trees, and a carp-filled pond linked by winding pathways. West of the Tea Garden a road encircles Stow Lake, at the center of which Strawberry Hill rises to a 400-foot summit.

HIGHLIGHTS

- Japanese Tea Garden
- Stow Lake

INFORMATION

- ✚ A/B/C/D/E/F 7/8
- ✉ Bordered by Great Highway, Lincoln Way, Fulton Street and Stanyan Street
- ☎ 415/666 7200
- ⏱ Always open; only daylight visiting is recommended
- 🍴 Excellent café (S) at M. H. De Young Memorial Museum; tea served at Japanese Tea Garden (S)
- 🚍 5, 7, 18, 21, 28, 29, 44, 71
- ♿ Good
- 🎟 Free
- ↔ Asian Art Museum (➤ 28) California Academy of Sciences (➤ 30), M. H. De Young Memorial Museum (➤ 29)
- ❓ Walking tours May–Oct ☎ 415/221 1311

One of the features of Golden Gate Park

3

PALACE OF THE LEGION OF HONOR

HIGHLIGHTS

- *Eiffel Tower,* Seurat
- *Water Lilies,* Monet
- *The Tribute Money,* Rubens
- *Saint John the Baptist,* El Greco
- *Thinker,* Rodin
- *The Shades,* Rodin
- *Holocaust* sculpture, Segal
- *Old Man and Old Woman,* De la Tour
- *Man With A Broken Nose,* Rodin
- View of Golden Gate

INFORMATION

- ✚ B5
- ✉ Lincoln Park
- ☎ 415/750 3600; recorded information ☎ 415/863 3330
- ◉ Wed–Sun 10–5; 10–8:45, first Wed in month. Closed Mon and Tue
- 🍴 Simple café (S)
- 🚌 18
- ♿ Good
- 💲 Moderate; ticket also valid at the Asian Art Museum and M. H. De Young Memorial Museum on same day. Free 10–12 noon first Wed and Sat of month
- ↔ Golden Gate National Recreation Area (► 24)
- ❓ Free tours daily

Rodin and San Francisco may seem an unlikely combination, but I suggest fans of the sculptor pay a visit to the hilltop site where a building modeled on the **Légion d'Honneur** *Museum in Paris displays many of his works amid a fine collection of European art.*

Sugar money The collection in the California Palace of the Legion of Honor was started in the 1910s by Alma Spreckels, wife of millionaire San Franciscan sugar magnate, Adolph. Already passionate about European art, Alma met Rodin in Paris and began a lasting interest in his work. Her husband, meanwhile, was motivated to open an art museum through his bitter rivalry with another prominent San Franciscan family, the De Youngs, who had founded the M. H. De Young Memorial Museum (► 29).

The collections *The Shades* and a *Thinker* stand in the grounds and some 70 other Rodin works are inside the museum. The general galleries, meanwhile, are arranged in a chronological sequence from the medieval period to the early 20th century, with the highlights mostly from the 18th and 19th centuries. Downstairs, the Achenbach Foundation for Graphic Arts holds over 100,000 prints and some 3,000 drawings from artists as diverse as Albrecht Dürer and Georgia O'Keeffe and selections are shown in short-term exhibitions (otherwise by appointment). Outside, beside the parking lot, be sure to see George Segal's *Holocaust* sculpture.

GOLDEN GATE BRIDGE

I defy anybody to suggest that San Francisco's Golden Gate Bridge is not the most instantly recognizable, and the most beautiful, of all the 575,000 bridges in the United States.

Artful engineering Named for the bay it crosses rather than its color, the bridge is a remarkable artistic as well as an engineering feat. The construction overcame the exceptional depth and strong currents of the Golden Gate, while a simple but inspired design allows it to sit with panache between the city and the wild hillsides of Marin County; its upper portions are often evocatively shrouded in fog.

Loathed then loved A bond issue of $35 million was authorized in 1930 to finance the bridge's construction amid great antipathy from San Franciscans, many of whom feared a loss of the natural beauty of the Golden Gate. An early design by the project's chief engineer, Joseph B. Strauss, was likened to "two grotesque steel beetles emerging from either bank." The design eventually adopted is thought to have been the work of one or more of Strauss's assistants. The affection that the bridge now enjoys among city dwellers was confirmed in 1987 when 200,000 people filed onto it to mark the 50th anniversary of its opening, causing the central span to drop by ten feet.

Fatal attraction On a more downbeat note, the Golden Gate Bridge has become a noted spot for suicides. The first occurred three months after the bridge's opening and, to date, almost 1,000 people have ended their lives by jumping the 220 feet from the central span to the raging waters beneath, their bodies usually carried out to the Pacific by the swift currents of the bay.

DID YOU KNOW?

- Weight of steel in construction: 100,000 tons
- Length including approaches: 7 miles
- Actual bridge length: 6,450 feet
- Length of central span: 4,200 feet
- Height above water: 220 feet at low tide
- Height of towers: 746 feet
- Length of cables: 80,000 miles
- Color: International Orange, the color most distinguishable in fog
- Gallons of paint used annually: 5,000
- Annual vehicle crossings: 42,000,000

INFORMATION

- D1/2/3
- 415/921 5858
- Open to pedestrians daily 5–9
- 28, 29, 76
- Good at observation platform
- Free for pedestrians and cyclists; moderate toll for city-bound drivers
- Golden Gate National Recreation Area (► 24)
- Guided walking tours run by Roger's Custom Tours (☎ 415/742 9611)

5

ASIAN ART MUSEUM

HIGHLIGHTS

- Xuande Era blue and white porcelain
- Ming Dynasty calligraphy and fan painting
- Japanese *netsuke*
- Edo-period Japanese screen paintings
- Magnin Jade Gallery
- Tibetan *thangkas* (religious paintings)
- Tibetan thigh-bone trumpet
- Tibetan three-headed Bon figure

INFORMATION

- ✚ E7
- ✉ Golden Gate Park
- ☎ 415/668 8921; recorded information
  ☎ 415/668 7855
- 🕐 Wed–Sun 10–4:45; 10–8:45, first Wed of month. Closed Mon and Tue
- 🍴 Excellent café (S) in M. H. De Young Memorial Museum
- 🚌 44
- ♿ Excellent
- 💲 Moderate; includes M. H. De Young Memorial Museum and California Palace of the Legion of Honor if visited on same day. Free 10–12 noon first Wed and Sat of month
- ↔ Golden Gate Park (➤ 25), California Academy of Sciences (➤ 30)
- ❓ Free tours daily. Lectures, films

A carved pillar in the museum

I guarantee that something amid the wealth of treasures inside the Asian Art Museum—the largest collection of its kind in the country—will catch your eye, be it Chinese jade, Japanese netsuke or a Tibetan thigh-bone trumpet.

The Brundage collection The museum originated with an immense collection of Asian artifacts assembled by the industrialist and former president of the International Olympic Committee, Avery Brundage. San Francisco, with its historic and cultural links with Asia, was chosen as the site of a museum to display the Brundage acquisitions. Since its opening in 1966 the museum has expanded its stock considerably. It now has 15,000 pieces and lacks the space to show more than a fraction of the holdings at one time.

Diverse exhibits With exhibits spanning 6,000 years and diverse cultures and religions, there is a lot to be said for simply wandering through the galleries, pausing at whatever grabs your attention. The major collections are from China and include the oldest dated example of Chinese Buddhist art (A.D. 338) and important items from the Ming Dynasty (1368–1644) and Xuande Era (1426–1435). But the smaller, less

obvious items can delight in equal measure, such as the wood carvings, silverwork, and textiles from Bhutan, which offer you a rare insight into this obscure country.

M. H. DE YOUNG MEMORIAL MUSEUM

From Anatolian prayer rugs to the dresses of Yves Saint-Laurent, the M. H. De Young Memorial Museum stocks many diverse exhibits from around the world, but I regard the exemplary collections of American painting and decorative art as being the main reason for a visit.

Paintings After society portraits by John Singleton Copley and his 18th-century contemporaries such as John Smibert, the paintings reveal the growing self-confidence of American artists and the lessening importance of European trends. By the mid-1800s, many American artists were taking inspiration from the newly settled American West: the landscapes of Albert Bierstadt and the sculpture of Frederick Remington both evoke the period's celebratory mood of expansion. Look out, too, for the entertaining room of *trompe-l'oeil* works, the most notable of the many clever canvases on display being the work of William Michael Harnett.

Furnishings The furniture collection, too, reflects America's historic shift from colony to nation, moving from English and Dutch armchairs used in New England settlements of 1670 to an elegant Federal-period parlor from 1805 Massachusetts. The flowing curves of the Queen Anne style were popular during the colonial period, but by the time of the Revolution American craftsmen had acquired the skills and creativity to evolve a new and distinctive look, adding unique rococo touches. Philadelphia emerged above Boston and New York as the center of the craft, and a grand 1780 Philadelphia high chest provides an excellent example of the period.

HIGHLIGHTS

- *Storm in the Rocky Mountains*, Bierstadt
- *A View of Donner Lake, California*, Bierstadt
- *The Ironworkers' Noontime*, Anshutz
- *Mrs. Daniel Sargent*, Copley
- *Marius amidst the ruins of Carthage*, Vanderlyn
- *After the Hunt*, Harnett
- *A Dinner Table at Night*, Singer Sargent
- Philadelphia high chest of drawers
- Paul Revere's silverware
- Shaker crafts

INFORMATION

- ✚ E7
- ✉ Golden Gate Park
- ☎ 415/750 3600; recorded information ☎ 415/863 3330
- ◷ Wed–Sun 10–4:45; 10–8:45, first Wed of month. Closed Mon and Tue
- 🍴 Excellent cafe (S)
- 🚍 44
- ♿ Excellent
- 💰 Moderate; includes Asian Art Museum and California Palace of the Legion of Honor if visited on same day. Free 10–12 noon first Wed and Sat of month.
- ↔ Golden Gate Park (▶ 25), Asian Art Museum (▶ 28),
- ❓ Free tours daily. Lectures, films

CALIFORNIA ACADEMY OF SCIENCES

HIGHLIGHTS

- Splitfin Flashlight fish
- Dolphins
- Safequake
- The Swamp
- Far Side of Science Gallery
- Life Through Time Gallery
- Morrison Planetarium
- Gem and Mineral Hall
- California Tidepool

INFORMATION

- E7
- Golden Gate Park
- 415/221 5100; recorded information 415/750 7145; Planetarium 415/750 7141; Laserium 415/750 7138
- Sep–Jun, daily 10–5; Jul–Aug, daily 10–7. Planetarium shows hourly Sat and Sun 1–4 (from 11 in summer), Mon–Fri 2PM. Laserium shows Thu–Sun evenings
- Reasonable café (S)
- 44
- Excellent
- Moderate; free first Wed of month
- Asian Art Museum (➤ 28) Golden Gate Park (➤ 25), M. H. De Young Memorial Museum (➤ 29)
- Free tours daily. Daily feeding: penguins 11:30 & 4; seals and dolphins every 2 hours, starting at 10:30 (no feeding on Wed). Lectures, films

If you have children with you, I would recommend particularly the California Academy of Sciences as part of a day spent in Golden Gate Park, if only to experience a Californian earthquake safely.

Strange creatures Founded in 1853 by a small group of enthusiasts who held weekly meetings and published papers on the state's newly discovered animal species, the California Academy of Sciences has evolved into a sizable museum. The exhibits give a thoroughly entertaining introduction to the natural world, an introduction that begins with a face-to-jaw encounter with a Great White shark, the most imposing exhibit in a room devoted to Californian dioramas. Living creatures in the Steinhart Aquarium include alligators, dolphins, penguins, and the mysterious Splitfin Flashlight fish, which uses the piscine equivalent of a flashlight to find its way around very deep, very dark waters.

Hi-tech history In other galleries, a fossilized stegosaurus tail spike sits next to the computers that allow visitors to trace evolutionary links through 3.5 billion years of history. The vibrating floor of the Safequake exhibit re-creates the earthquakes that rocked San Francisco's streets in 1865 and 1906. The Gem and Mineral Hall displays plenty of remarkable rocks, including an amethyst-lined geode and nuggets of Californian gold. The Morrison Planetarium, meanwhile, offers narrated voyages to Black Holes and other oddities of the cosmos, and several evenings each week stages a laserium show that creates phantasmagorical visual images to a musical accompaniment. As a final treat, allow ample time to study and enjoy the Far Side of Science Gallery, where 159 of Gary Larson's hilarious science-inspired cartoons line the walls.

Neptune Society Columbarium

One way I convince San Franciscans that I know more about their home town than they do is by telling them about the Neptune Society Columbarium. It is among the city's most historically and architecturally noteworthy buildings, but one of which most locals are unaware.

The moving dead An elegant, three-story Victorian rotunda decorated with stained glass, the Columbarium (a final resting place for urns holding the ashes of the deceased) was designed by British architect Bernard Cahill and was opened in 1898. By 1937, it stood in the heart of a three-acre cemetery in which an estimated 10,000 people were buried. That year, however, concerns about public health resulted in cemeteries being declared illegal in San Francisco; the graves were exhumed and their contents moved out of the city.

The interior of the Columbarium

Notable niches Declared a memorial, the Columbarium itself was spared demolition but, with cremations being outlawed, found itself without a purpose and was left to decay. Restoration of the handsome structure began in 1980, and its empty niches were once again put on sale. Guided tours focus on the architecture, but even a swift glance at the niches will reveal Eddys, Turks, and other once illustrious families who gave their names to city streets.

DID YOU KNOW?

- Architect: Bernard Cahill
- Year completed: 1898
- Original owners: Oddfellows Cemetery
- Owners since 1980: Neptune Society of Northern California
- Other owners: Bay City Cemeteries Association (1930), Cypress Abbey (1935)
- Number of niches: 30,000
- Number of unoccupied niches: 10,000
- Most expensive currently available niche: $56,000
- Least expensive currently available niche: $700
- Most unusual niche adornment: a set of miniature golf clubs

INFORMATION

- ✚ F6
- ✉ 1 Loraine Court
- ☎ 415/221 1838
- ◷ Mon–Fri 9–1; Sat and Sun 10–1
- 🚌 33, 38, 50
- ♿ None
- 💲 Free
- ↔ Asian Art Museum (➤ 28), California Academy of Sciences (➤ 30), Golden Gate Park (➤ 25), M. H. De Young Memorial Museum (➤ 29), Temple Emanu-El (➤ 52).
- ❓ Tours Sat 10 and 11:30

31

EXPLORATORIUM

INFORMATION

- G3
- 3601 Lyon Street
- 415/563 7337; recorded information 415/561 0360; Tactile Dome reservations 415/561 0362
- Sep–May, Tue–Sun, 10–5 Wed, 10–9:30. Jun–Aug, daily 10–6
- Reasonable cafeteria ($)
- 28, 30
- Excellent
- Moderate; free first Wed of month. Tactile Dome: moderate separate fee
- Palace of Fine Arts (► 33), Marina Green (► 56)

The Exploratorium is undoubtedly the best place in San Francisco to amuse young minds with low boredom thresholds and is no less pleasurable for adults; I for one have spent many hours absorbed in its engaging and entertaining midst.

Questions and answers Founded by Frank Oppenheimer, who worked alongside his more famous brother, Robert, on the development of the atomic bomb in the 1940s, the Exploratorium occupies a single vast hall and has 650 hands-on, interactive exhibits designed to illustrate and explain the fundamentals of natural science and human perception in a user-friendly environment. Helpful red-jacketed "explainers" stroll around answering questions, and new exhibits are developed in a workshop open to public view. The odd bits of statuary you might spot gathering dust in the corners are remnants of the building's original role as part of the Palace of Fine Arts (► 33).

Innovative art and science Be they crackling tesla coils or coupled resonant pendulums, the exhibits stand alongside the results of an innovative artist-in-residence program that produced Ned Kahn's *Tornado*, a reservoir of fog continually pulled upwards in an inverted vortex, and Paul de Marinis' *Alien Voices*, that allows two people in separate wooden telephone booths to speak to each other in a choice of 16 computer-altered voices. The Golden Gate videodisc simulates the experience of hovering above San Francisco, while the Exploratorium's most popular item (and one that requires a reservation) is the Tactile Dome, a dark space from which participants can leave only by feeling their way out on their hands and knees.

PALACE OF FINE ARTS

Together with the Golden Gate Bridge and City Hall, the Palace of Fine Arts is, for me, one of the most beautiful structures in San Francisco. Remarkably, it was intentionally built as a ruin and serves no practical purpose whatsoever.

Architects' playtime In 1915, ostensibly to mark the opening of the Panama Canal, San Francisco announced its recovery from the devastation of the 1906 earthquake and fire by staging the Panama Pacific International Exposition. A group of noted architects was commissioned to erect temporary structures to house the Expo on land reclaimed from the bay. One of the architects was Bernard Maybeck, and it was his Palace of Fine Arts more than any other building that captured the imagination of the Expo's 20 million visitors. Although it was intended as a temporary structure and was built mostly of plaster and chicken-wire, the Palace of Fine Arts aroused such public affection that it was preserved and then, in the 1960s, replicated in concrete at a cost of $7.5 million.

Art in ruins Maybeck designed a Roman ruin, using a classical domed rotunda as the structure's centerpiece and flanking this with a fragmented colonnade. Each group of columns was topped by weeping maidens and decorated by aimless stairways and funeral urns. The intention was to instill a sense of "moderated sadness" and to prepare visitors for the classical art exhibited in the Expo's Great Hall (now housing the Exploratorium ➤ 32). Far from making one sad, however, the palace is mysterious and enchanting, an effect greatly aided by the building's reflection in the reposeful, duck-filled lagoon that lies alongside.

DID YOU KNOW?

- Architect: Bernard Maybeck
- Built: 1915
- Inspirations: Böcklin's *Isle of the Dead*; the drawings of Piranesi
- Materials: originally plaster and wood on a chicken-wire frame
- Height of rotunda: 132 feet
- Restoration begun: 1962
- Restoration completed: 1975
- Original cost: $400,000

INFORMATION

- ✚ G3/4
- ✉ 3601 Lyon Street
- 🕐 Always open
- 🚌 28, 30
- ♿ None
- 🎫 Free
- ↔ Exploratorium (➤ 32), Marina Green (➤ 56)
- ❓ City Guides (☎ 415/557 4266) free walking tour usually twice monthly

MISSION DOLORES

DID YOU KNOW?

- Full name: Mission San Francisco de Asís
- Founded: 1776
- Building commenced: 1782
- Building completed: 1791
- Length: 114 feet
- Width: 22 feet
- Thickness of walls: 4 feet
- Number of adobe bricks: 36,000
- Number of baptisms: 28,000
- First earthquake-proofing measures: 1918

INFORMATION

- ✚ H/J8
- ✉ 320 Dolores Street (entrance on 16th Street)
- ☎ 415/621 8203
- ⊙ May–Oct, daily 9–4:30; Nov–Apr, daily 9–4
- 🚌 22, J
- ♿ Few
- 💲 Inexpensive
- ↔ The Castro (➤ 51), Levi Strauss Factory (➤ 55), Mission District (➤ 50)
- ❓ Occasional mass held in chapel

Evidence of the 18th-century Spanish settlement of California rarely surfaces in today's San Francisco, but Mission Dolores, founded in 1776 and the oldest intact building in the city, provides a welcome, if modest, insight into the era.

California's missions Completed in 1791, the mission was the sixth in a chain of 21 built by the Spanish across California. From San Diego in the south to Sonoma in the north, each mission was located a day's horse-ride from the next. The Spaniards' intention was to convert Native Americans to Catholicism, to utilize their labor, and to earn their support in any colonial conflict. Mexico's independence from Spain in 1821 put the sparsely populated California in Mexican hands, and resulted in the decline and secularization of many of the missions. Most were restored under U.S. rule, many as a job-creation program in the 1930s during the Depression.

Inside the mission Passing through the thick adobe walls, largely responsible for the mission's success in withstanding numerous earthquakes, visitors first enter the small and richly atmospheric chapel, which holds an altar dating from 1780 and is decorated by frescoes executed by Native Americans. A modest assortment of historic pieces is gathered in the mission's museum, the oldest being a baptismal register for 1776. In the mission's cemetery, headstones mark Spanish- and Mexican-era notables, while the Lourdes Grotto indicates the common grave of some 5,000 Native Americans. A door from the mission leads into the grandiose parish church, raised beside the mission in 1918 and designated a basilica by the Pope in 1952.

FORT MASON CENTER

I think it is typical of San Francisco that the bleak exteriors of a set of former army barracks on the city's northern waterfront now hold more than 50 diverse arts centers, theaters, galleries, and small museums.

From arms to art From the time of San Francisco's 18th-century Spanish *presidio* (or garrison) to the Korean War of the 1950s, Fort Mason served a military role. From 1972, however, the troop barracks were steadily transformed into a vibrant cultural center that still continues to expand. A recent addition is the innovative San Francisco Museum of Modern Art Rental Gallery.

Museums The Center's small museums with their various temporary exhibitions provide the main visitor appeal. They include the African-American Historical and Cultural Center and Museo Italo-Americano, focusing on black American and Italian-American topics respectively, and the San Francisco Craft and Folk Art Museum. The largest and best, however, is the Mexican Museum, where space limitations result in only a tiny selection of 9,000 items being on show, with the emphasis instead on often provocative short-term exhibitions of contemporary Hispanic art.

HIGHLIGHTS

- Mexican Museum
- San Francisco Craft and Folk Art Museum
- African-American Historical and Cultural Center
- Museo Italo-Americano
- Magic Theater
- SS *Jeremiah O'Brien*
- Greens Restaurant
- Book Bay
- San Francisco Museum of Modern Art Rental Gallery
- Cowell Theater

INFORMATION

- ✚ H/J3
- ✉ Marina Boulevard at Laguna Street
- ☎ 415/441 5706
- 🕐 Individual museums vary
- 🍴 The excellent Greens vegetarian restaurant ($$$) and the adjoining Tassajara bakery ($)
- 🚌 22, 28, 30, 49
- ♿ Few
- 💲 Individual museums free or inexpensive
- ↔ Ghirardelli Square (► 54); Golden Gate National Recreation Area (► 24), Hyde Street Pier Historical Ships (► 39), Marina Green (► 56), National Maritime Museum (► 53), Octagon House (► 55)
- ❓ Numerous special events

The San Francisco Craft and Folk Art Museum

St. Mary's Cathedral

I had seen the striking modern architecture of St. Mary's Cathedral on many occasions before I realized what I was looking at, its towering, gleaming white hyperbolic paraboloids being distinctly visible from across a wide section of the city. A closer inspection should not be missed.

Undivided worship The paraboloids give the cathedral a 190-feet-high ceiling and form the shape of a Greek cross. Inside, the open-plan cathedral (formally St. Mary's Catholic Cathedral of the Assumption) can seat 2,400 people. Its design is intended to eliminate the usual divisions between a cathedral's different areas. Here, the apse, nave, transepts, baptistery, and narthex are undivided beneath the tall ceiling, in the center of which is a skylight in the shape of the Cross. The four stained-glass windows that rise from floor to ceiling in each main wall represent the four elements.

Cathedrals past The cathedral could hardly provide a greater contrast with its predecessor, now known as Old St. Mary's Church, which stands in Chinatown. Old St. Mary's opened as the first Catholic cathedral on the West Coast and served the city until 1891. In that year, a new St. Mary's took on the role until 1962, when it was destroyed by fire. Curiously, the present cathedral stands on a plot of land previously occupied by a supermarket, demolished to make way for the modernistic religious edifice.

The striking interior of St. Mary's Cathedral

14

CITY HALL

The crowning glory of the Civic Center complex, City Hall is a beaux-arts masterpiece and seems an entirely fitting place for San Francisco to conduct its day-to-day administrative affairs.

A symbol City Hall's immense rotunda is topped by a green copper dome (modeled on St. Peter's in Rome) visible across much of the city. This intricate and inspiring building at the heart of San Francisco was completed in 1915 and arose from the drawing-boards of architects Arthur Brown and John Bakewell. Both architects studied at the École des Beaux Arts in Paris at a time when the classically inspired City Beautiful movement, which began in the 1890s, was greatly influencing American urban planning. In San Francisco, the authorities were eager for a building to symbolize San Francisco's superiority over fast-growing Los Angeles. It was Brown and Bakewell's plan—based on the French baroque style, making free use of marble and with barely a square inch not graced with some form of decoration—that won the day. Because of earthquake damage and a restoration program, City Hall was closed to the public in the mid-1990s and its office workers moved to other buildings in the city. It is scheduled to reopen in 1998.

Interior When the building is reopened to the public, it will once again be possible to go inside and climb the grand staircase, lined by ornate wrought-iron banisters and illuminated by free-standing and hanging lamps, and idle around the landings where porticoes and arches, topped by neoclassical sculptured guardians, give access to the labyrinthine complex of offices and official chambers.

DID YOU KNOW?

- Architects: Brown & Bakewell
- Prize for winning design competition: $25,000
- Building cost: $3.5 million
- Year completed: 1915
- Height of dome: 300 feet
- Occupants: mayor, elected for four-year term, and Board of Supervisors, the 11-member city legislature
- Assassination: Mayor George Moscone and Supervisor Harvey Milk, 1978
- Weddings: many, including, in 1980, that of Mayor Dianne Feinstein who invited the entire city to attend
- Previous land use: cemetery

INFORMATION

- ✚ J6
- ✉ 400 Van Ness Avenue
- ☎ 415/554 4000
- 🕐 Closed at present
- 🍴 None
- 🚇 Civic Center or Van Ness
- 🚌 5, 10, 20, 21, 42, 47, 49, 60, 70, 80
- ♿ Good
- 🎫 Free
- ↔ St. Mary's Cathedral (➤ 36), Levi Strauss Factory (➤ 55)

37

ALCATRAZ

As much a part of San Francisco as the Golden Gate Bridge or cable cars, the former prison of Alcatraz sits on an island in San Francisco Bay and is far and away the city's strangest sight—yet one that nobody should miss.

DID YOU KNOW?

- Named: Isla de los Alcatraces (Island of Pelicans), 1775
- Island size: 22½ acres
- Number of prisoners 1,576
- Number of cells: 450
- Cell size 10 feet by 4 feet

INFORMATION

- ✚ J1
- ✉ San Francisco Bay
- ☎ 415/546 2700
- ⏲ Daily, according to first and last ferries
- 🚢 Red & White Fleet from Pier 41, Fisherman's Wharf
- ♿ Few
- 🍴 Moderate; advance booking advised in summer
- ❓ Self-guided audio tours recommended; moderate

No escape A mile and a half north of Fisherman's Wharf and easily sighted from any high vantage point in the city, Alcatraz became the country's most feared place of incarceration from 1934, after the federal government took control of the island. It was turned into a top-security penitentiary for "incorrigible" criminals—those deemed beyond salvation and considered too dangerous to be held at conventional jails. There was one guard for every three inmates, work was a privilege that had to be earned through good behavior, and prisoners who did escape from their cells were faced with the prospect of crossing the freezing, swiftly moving waters of the bay (regarded as unswimmable) to freedom. Known escape attempts number 36; five escapees are unaccounted for and can perhaps be counted as successful.

Moody viewing The former cells, mess hall, hospital, and exercise yard are all open for viewing, and an audio-cassette tour with a terse commentary by former Alcatraz guards and inmates makes an excellent atmospheric accompaniment. The costs and difficulties of running an island prison, and public disquiet at the severity of the regime, contributed to Alcatraz's closure in 1963. A small museum traces the broader history of the island, that was claimed and occupied by Native Americans in 1964 for two years under an 1868 treaty that granted them rights to "unused government land".

This cell in Alcatraz was featured in the movie Escape from Alcatraz

HYDE STREET PIER HISTORICAL SHIPS

San Francisco was long the hub of the West Coast's maritime trade, and the vessels permanently docked at Hyde Street Pier, as part of the National Maritime Museum, provide an enjoyable reminder of the city's seafaring heyday and its dependence on waterborne travel before the building of the bay bridges.

Cape Horn veteran The grandest of the ships is the *Balclutha*, a steel-hulled, square-rigged ship launched in Scotland in 1886. The *Balclutha*, originally intended to carry grain between California and Europe, rounded Cape Horn several times before ending its days transporting Alaskan salmon along the West Coast. Clamber down the ladders and around the decks for a look at the restored cabins, including the elegant saloon enjoyed by the ship's Master, and to scrutinize the informative explanatory texts.

Boats of the bay The 1940s cars and trucks on the lower decks of the *Eureka* suggest the era when the vessel was the world's largest passenger ferry and able to haul more than 2,000 people and 100 vehicles between San Francisco and Sausalito in a single trip. The other exhibits are the *C.A. Thayer*, built in 1895 to move the lumber used in the construction of many early Californian cities; a 1907 deep-water steam tug, *Hercules*; the *Wapama*, built in 1915 and the last survivor of 235 Californian steam schooners; a paddle-tug dating from 1914, *Eppleton Hall*, which spent its working life towing coal ships and barges in Britain; and the dainty *Alma*, a scow schooner (a type of sail-powered cargo barge) whose flat bottom enabled her to navigate with ease the shallow waters on the periphery of the bay.

HIGHLIGHTS

- *Balclutha*
- *Eureka*
- *C.A. Thayer*
- *Alma*
- *Wapama*
- *Eppleton Hall*
- Maritime Bookstore

INFORMATION

- ✚ J3
- ✉ Aquatic Park, foot of Hyde Street
- ☎ 415/556 3002
- 🕐 Mid-May–mid-Sep, daily 10–6; mid-Sep–mid-May, daily 9:30–5
- 🚌 19, 32; Hyde–Powell cable car
- ♿ None
- 🎟 Moderate; free on first Tue of month
- ↔ Fort Mason Center (▶ 35), Ghirardelli Square (▶ 54), National Maritime Museum (▶ 53)
- ❓ Occasional ranger-led tours, periodic special events

17

GRACE CATHEDRAL

HIGHLIGHTS

- Ghiberti doors
- Chapel of Grace
- Stained-glass windows
- Rose window
- Gobelin tapestry

INFORMATION

- K5
- 1051 Taylor Street
- 415/776 6611
- Usually daily 7:30–6
- 1; California Street cable car
- Good
- Cable Car Museum (▶41), Fairmont Hotel (▶57), Huntington Park (▶56), Nob Hill (▶50), Old St. Mary's Church (▶52)
- Free tours daily, usually before and after services. Occasional lectures, exhibitions on social issues

I like to think that Grace Cathedral, located as it is on the site of a former robber-baron's Nob Hill mansion, provides some spiritual atonement for the materialist excesses that characterize the neighborhood.

Slow building When the mansion of railroad boss Charles Crocker (▶12) was destroyed by the fire that followed San Francisco's 1906 earthquake, the Crocker family donated its plot to the Episcopalian church. Although the cathedral's cornerstone was laid in 1910, construction did not begin until 1928 and further delays, due partly to the Depression, resulted in Grace Cathedral's consecration being delayed until 1964. Described by its main architect, Lewis P. Hobart, as "a truly American cathedral," Grace Cathedral is in fact neo-Gothic in style, partly modeled on Notre Dame in Paris.

Through the doors The most impressive exterior feature is a pair of gilded bronze doors from the Lorenzo Ghiberti cast used for the Gates of Paradise doors of the Baptistery in Florence. Inside, a 15th-century French altarpiece and an exquisite Flemish reredos can be seen in the Chapel of Grace, while the stained-glass windows depict biblical scenes and diverse achievers such as Albert Einstein and Henry Ford. The cathedral has, controversially, frequently invited radical figures to speak from the pulpit.

Grace Cathedral took more than 50 years to build

CABLE CAR MUSEUM

The ring of the cable car bell provides a constant reminder that you are in San Francisco, probably the only city in the world where a relatively inefficient form of public transportation is adored by the entire population.

Inspired Legend has it that a horse, falling while trying to drag its load up a San Franciscan hill, inspired Andrew Smith Hallidie—a Scots-born manufacturer of wire rope who arrived in California in 1852—to invent the cable car. Wire rope had previously been used as a means of transporting materials in gold mines, but Hallidie was the first to develop the idea as a means of moving people. Besides improving transportation throughout the city, the cable car facilitated the settlement of Nob Hill. Damage caused by the 1906 earthquake and fire, and the subsequent rise of motorized transportation, soon rendered cable cars obsolete. Pressure from San Franciscans led the federal government to award National Historic Landmark status to cable cars in 1964, however, and a provision in the city's charter ensures the preservation of the three remaining lines.

Simple but effective The museum's intriguing memorabilia, including the first cable car, tell the story of the system's development. The clever engineering principle that keeps the cars running is also revealed: each one is pulled by an underground cable that never stops moving. The "gripman" on each car uses a lever to connect or disconnect the car to or from the cable through a slot in the road. The whirring sound, audible as you enter the museum, is the noise made by the steel cable being pulled over 14-feet-wide winding wheels, a process visible in the museum's lower level.

DID YOU KNOW?

- First cable car run: August 2, 1873
- First route: Clay Street
- Most cars in use: 600
- Most miles of track: 112
- Current number of cars in use: 38
- Current miles of track: 11
- Depth of cable beneath street: 18 inches
- Width of cable: 1¼ inches
- Average speed of cable car: 9½mph
- Annual cable car passengers: 10,500,000

INFORMATION

- K4
- 1201 Mason Street
- 415/474 1887
- Apr–Oct, daily 10–6; Nov–Mar, daily 10–5
- 1, 30, 45, 83; Powell–Mason, Powell–Hyde cable cars
- Few; good on lower level
- Free
- Bank of Canton (➤55), Chinatown (➤50), Fairmont Hotel (➤57), Grace Cathedral (➤40), Huntington Park (➤56), Ina Coolbrith Park (➤56), Nob Hill (➤50), North North Beach Museum (➤53), Old St. Mary's Church (➤52), Tien Hou Temple (➤52), Waverly Place (➤60)

ANSEL ADAMS CENTER

Those who doubt the power of photography to provide social comment and to raise questions about the world are well advised to visit the Ansel Adams Center, an outstanding showplace for enquiring and creative picture-taking. **"**

The exhibitions The Center's five galleries stage around 15 exhibitions each year and at any given time the combined displays offer an absorbing and sometimes provocative blend of historical and contemporary work. Photographers from the United States and overseas, household names and comparative unknowns—all are represented, variously using the camera's ability to read faces, exploit juxtapositions, and even make landscapes resonate with emotion. Past exhibitions have ranged from Eadweard Muybridge's extraordinary panoramas of 1880s San Francisco, to Wendy Ewald's work in urban and rural communities of Mexico giving local children the opportunity to photograph themselves, their environment and their community.

Photographic friends The Center is named after the award-winning photographer whose evocative landscapes, particularly those of Yosemite Valley and of the other national parks, encouraged the preservation of some of the country's most celebrated areas of natural beauty and encouraged countless other photographers to aim their lenses at the features of nature. In 1967, together with Brett Weston (the photographer son of a photographer father Edward Weston) and art critic Beaumont Newhall, Adams founded the Friends of Photography, an organization whose workshops earned a reputation for encouraging exploration of the camera's creative potential. The Friends currently run the Center.

CHINESE HISTORICAL SOCIETY OF AMERICA

The Chinese have been present for longer, and in greater numbers, than any other non–Anglo ethnic group in San Francisco, greatly contributing to the city's multicultural character.

Early days The Chinese arrived in California in force during the Gold Rush, but met racial hostility and the foreigners tax (ostensibly due from all non-U.S. citizens in California, but in practice only levied against the Chinese). They were unjustly blamed for the economic depression that followed the gold boom and were eventually forced into "Chinatown" communities, the largest being in San Francisco. With further immigration outlawed and the Manchu dynasty exercising strict control over Chinese people both at home and overseas, Chinatown became populated almost exclusively by males who wore traditional dress and tied their hair in braids. Denied the comforts of traditional family life, many Chinese men gambled, smoked opium, joined the secret Chinese-American societies known as Tongs, and visited prostitutes to alleviate the boredom —activities that added to the area's mystique.

Recent times Not until the founding of the Chinese Republic in 1911 were the Chinese able to adopt western ideas and modes of dress. By the 1920s, the restaurants and stores of Chinatown were becoming tourist attractions and the Chinese, expanded in numbers through the easing of immigration restrictions, steadily became an accepted part of city life. This tiny museum does an excellent job in outlining the story of the Chinese in California, with many revealing texts alongside exhibits that range from gold-mining paraphernalia and religious objects to a 19th-century opium pipe.

DID YOU KNOW?

- Chinese in California, 1851: 25,000
- Chinese employed on transcontinental railroad, late 1860s: 10,000
- Proportion of factory jobs held by Chinese in San Francisco in 1872: 50%
- Chinese in San Francisco in 1875: 46,000
- Chinese in San Francisco in 1882: 26,000
- Number of Chinatown opium dens, 1885: 26
- Chinese in San Francisco in 1900: 11,000
- Chinese immigrants to San Francisco 1910-40: 175,000
- Estimated Chinese-Americans in San Francisco today: 90,000

INFORMATION

- ✚ L4
- ✉ 650 Commercial Street
- ☎ 415/391 1188
- 🕐 Tue–Sat 12–4
- 🚍 1, 15, 41
- ♿ None
- 🎟 Free
- ↔ Bank of Canton (➤ 55), Chinatown (➤ 50), North Beach Museum (➤ 53), Old St. Mary's Church (➤ 52), Tien Hou Temple (➤ 52), Transamerica Pyramid (➤ 45), Transamerica Redwood Park (➤ 56), Waverly Place (➤ 60)

SAN FRANCISCO MUSEUM OF MODERN ART

HIGHLIGHTS

- *Woman with the Hat*, Matisse
- *Head in Three-quarter View*, Picasso
- *The Coffee Pot*, Picasso
- *Guardians of the Secret*, Pollock
- *Violin and Candlestick*, Braque
- Paul Klee drawings
- Charles and Ray Eames office furniture
- *The Flower Carrier*, Rivera
- Clyfford Still gallery
- East European photography

INFORMATION

- ✚ L5
- ✉ 151 Third Street
- ☎ 415/357 4000
- ⏰ Tue–Sun 11–6; until 9 on Thu. Closed Mon
- 🍴 Good café ($)
- 🚌 12, 15, 30, 45, 76
- ♿ Excellent
- 💲 Moderate; free first Tue of month
- ↔ Ansel Adams Center (➤ 42), Cartoon Art Museum (➤ 53), Marriott Hotel (➤ 54), Pacific Telephone Building (➤ 55), SoMa (➤ 51), Telephone Pioneer Communications Museum (➤ 59)
- ❓ Free tours daily. Lectures, films, other events

One of the few things I used to dislike about San Francisco was its lack of a world-class modern art museum—a state of affairs ended in January 1995 by the opening of the excellent new San Francisco Museum of Modern Art.

Second floor The core of the museum's permanent collections is shown in the second-floor galleries, which highlight painting and sculpture from 1900 to 1970. Among significant contributions from Europeans are Pablo Picasso's *Head in Three-quarter View* and *The Coffee Pot* and Georges Braque's *Violin and Candlestick*. Be sure not to miss the museum's prize possession: Matisse's *Woman with the Hat*, painted in 1905 and a work that made a crucial contribution to what became the century's first radical art movement, Fauvism. A striking complement of abstract expressionist canvases includes Jackson Pollock's *Guardians of the Secret*, contributions from Willem de Kooning, and the last work by color-field painter, Barnett Newman. Latin American artists are also given prominent space; among the best represented are the intriguing Mexican Modernists, Diego Rivera, and Frida Kahlo.

Other galleries With 17,000 exhibits spread across six floors and over 200,000 square feet, the museum has the space to devote several special galleries to California Art. In this section the canvases of Richard Diebenkorn, especially the artist's long-running Ocean Park series, have particular impact and relevance to the region, as do the 28 works donated by California-based abstract expressionist Clyfford Still. The museum is also equipped to stage provocative exhibitions in the emerging fields of video, computer, and interactive art.

TRANSAMERICA PYRAMID

The Transamerica Pyramid is San Francisco's most distinctive building and arguably the most innovative modern contribution to the city's skyline. Stepping inside is hard to resist although doing so may prove to be somewhat anticlimactic.

Perfect profile San Franciscans were slow to appreciate the splendor of the 853-feet-high building's unique profile, rising above the Financial District's forest of even-sided high-rises with a slowly-tapering spire flanked by windowless wings and with a decorative spire rising for 212 feet above the 48th floor. Yet the Transamerica Pyramid adds greatly to the city skyline and has steadily been accepted since 1972. The building is particularly appealing at night, when the hollow spire is lit from within and casts a distinctive glow above the city.

Inside looking out The building is a place of work for the 1,500 employees of the 50 firms (most of them financial) who rent its office space. The owners, the Transamerica Corporation, grew from various companies built around the Bank of Italy (later renamed the Bank of America) established in San Francisco in 1904. Although various works of art are arranged around the first floor, the interior of the building holds little of interest save for the Observation Level on the 27th floor, which offers views to North Beach and beyond.

DID YOU KNOW?

- Architect: William L Pereira & Associates
- Smallest floor: 48th, 45 feet per side
- Largest floor: 5th, 145 feet per side
- Angle of slope: 5 degrees
- Depth of excavation: 52 feet
- Number of floors: 48

INFORMATION

- ✛ L4
- ✉ 600 Montgomery Street
- ☎ No visitor phone
- 🍽 Average restaurant ground floor (SS)
- 🕐 Mon–Fri 8:30–4:30
- 🚌 15, 41
- ♿ Good
- 🎫 Free
- ↔ Bank of America HQ (➤ 54), Bank of Canton (➤ 55), Chinatown (➤ 50), Chinese Historical Society of America (➤ 43), Old St. Mary's Church (➤ 52), Tien Hou Temple (➤ 52), Transamerica Redwood Park (➤ 56), Waverly Place (➤ 60), Wells Fargo Museum (➤ 46)

WELLS FARGO MUSEUM

The company may have grown into one of the leading U.S. financial institutions, but for me the name of Wells Fargo is synonymous with the early days of the American West, and this collection ably demonstrates the historic links.

Going west Having established an express mail service in the East by the 1840s, Henry Wells and William G. Fargo began viewing the opportunities offered by Gold-Rush-era California with relish and opened an office in San Francisco in 1852. Whether buying, selling, or transporting gold, transferring funds or delivering mail, the company earned a reputation for trustworthiness in an era dominated by rogues. By 1861, Wells Fargo & Co. was operating the western leg of the famed Pony Express (which ran for only 18 months) and, by the late 1860s, monopolized the movement of mail across the western United States. In 1905 the mail delivery and banking divisions of the company were separated, when the latter combined with the Nevada Bank—founded by the San Francisco-based silver barons of the Comstock Lode—setting Wells Fargo on the path to becoming a major player in the world of American high finance.

Looking back A few steps from the site of the company's 1852 office, the Wells Fargo Museum (inside the Wells Fargo Bank) entertainingly documents the rise of the company. Sitting inside an 1860s stagecoach provides one highlight, but there is much more to see amid the clutter of a re-created Gold-Rush-era Wells Fargo office: gold-weighing scales, bulky mining tools, gold coins, and numerous aging letters that miraculously survived their trip across the rutted tracks of the old West.

24

THE OAKLAND MUSEUM

If you only make one crossing of San Francisco Bay, make it to Oakland where the Oakland Museum of Californian Art, Ecology, and History leads the way in documenting the extraordinary nature, history and art of the Golden State.

Nature The remarkable plant and animal life found in the high mountains, low deserts, and other habitats of California, are revealed by the 38,000-square-feet Hall of Ecology's elaborate dioramas. The adjoining Aquatic California Gallery does a similar job for underwater life, illustrating the goings-on in California's rivers, bays and hot springs, and beneath the ocean.

History Every episode in California's past is remembered here, thoughtfully explored and copiously documented. The collections are enhanced by interactive computers offering detailed information on particular exhibits, recorded commentaries from experts, and oral histories. From outlining the conflicts between indigenous Californians and the colonizing Spaniards, the collections come up to date with the rise of Californian computer companies and the invention of the mountain bike.

Californian art An imaginative selection of exhibits on the top floor of the museum demonstrates how the art of California has developed from 19th-century depictions of its untamed, natural beauty, through to the self-confidence of later 20th-century Californian artists such as semi-abstract painter Richard Diebenkorn and ceramicist Peter Voulkos. The photography collection includes outstanding contributions from Dorothea Lange and Maynard Dixon, both of whom were based in San Francisco.

HIGHLIGHTS

- *Yosemite Valley*, Bierstadt
- *Migrant Mother*, Lange
- Re-created Nevada City assay office
- Re-created "beatnik" coffee house
- Ness's custom motorcycles
- *California Miner with Packhorse*, Raschen
- *San Francisco, July 1849*, Davis

INFORMATION

- ⊞ Off map
- ✉ 1000 Oak Street, Oakland
- ☎ 510/238 3401; recorded information 510/834 2413
- ◷ Wed–Sat 10–5; Sun 12–7. Closed Mon and Tue
- ⑪ Good café (S)
- ◎ Lake Merritt
- ♿ Excellent
- ⊞ Moderate donation requested
- ❓ Free tours. Films, lectures, and events

BERKELEY CAMPUS

HIGHLIGHTS

- Sproul Plaza
- Sather Tower (also called the Campanile—carillon recitals on Sunday afternoons)
- Hearst Mining Building
- Phoebe A. Hearst Museum of Anthropology
- University Art Museum
- Sather Gate
- Lawrence Hall of Science
- Morrison Library
- Bancroft Library

INFORMATION

- ✚ Off map
- ✉ Main Gate, Bancroft Way
- ☎ 510/642 INFO; tour information 510/642 5215
- ◷ Daylight hours recommended
- ⵘ None, but many good options close by
- ⊠ Berkeley
- ⚹ Good
- ⊞ Free
- ❓ Free tours twice daily Mon, Wed and Fri

Children play on the DNA model on Berkeley campus

A haven of 1960s student dissent, the Berkeley campus might be less radical than it once was, but its buildings and museums and the picture it provides of contemporary Californian student life easily justify a trip.

Past The first college at Berkeley opened in the 1850s, but a lack of funds allowed the facility to be purchased in 1873 by the state government as the first of what are now six campuses of the University of California. Much of the university's early finance came as donations from Phoebe Apperson Hearst, wife of a wealthy mining baron and mother of the even more wealthy publishing tycoon, William Randolph Hearst. In the 1940s, Robert Oppenheimer was Berkeley's professor of physics before moving to Los Alamos to work on the first atomic bomb. In 1964, the seeds of what evolved into country-wide student rebellions were sown by the sit-ins and rallies of Berkeley's Free Speech Movement.

Present Nowadays, Berkeley's 30,000 students are more concerned with acquiring a good degree than immersing themselves in radical politics, though there is no shortage of causes and campaigns being promoted along Sproul Plaza, in the heart of the campus, on any week-day lunchtime. Elsewhere around the 100-acre campus is a selection of museums, libraries, and architecturally distinguished buildings such as John Galen Howard's *beaux-arts*-style Hearst Mining Building. Galen was also responsible for the elegant Sather Gate, which marks the main entrance to the campus opposite Telegraph Avenue.

SAN
FRANCISCO's
best

NEIGHBORHOODS

Fisherman's Wharf

Directly north of North Beach, Fisherman's Wharf is the only section of San Francisco pitched squarely at visitors. Former factories and fishing piers have been carefully and imaginatively converted to complexes of stores, restaurants, and tourist attractions. Despite the obvious commercial trappings, Fisherman's Wharf draws 12 million visitors each year and is, for most, an enjoyable experience.

A street in Chinatown

CHINATOWN

The compact streets and alleyways of Chinatown's 24 history-laden blocks are home to one of the largest Asian communities outside Asia. Several hundred-year-old temples, fortune-cookie factories, and numerous exotic stores are crammed into one of the city's most energetic and ethnically distinct neighborhoods. The area holds some of its best-value restaurants, inexpensive and excellent almost without fail.

✚ K/L 4/5 🚌 1, 15, 30, 45, 83; California Street cable car

HAIGHT-ASHBURY

Holding hundreds of elegant Victorian homes that survived the 1906 earthquake and fire, and becoming world-famous as the heart of hippiedom in 1967, Haight-Ashbury has long been the most tolerant section of a tolerant city. It holds exceptional used-bookstores and vintage clothing outlets and remains a lively center for alternative arts, culture, and lifestyles.

✚ F/G/H 6/7/8 🚌 6, 7, 24, 33, 43, 66, 71

JAPANTOWN

A concentration of Japanese temples, stores, and restaurants, and Japanese-style residential architecture, make this the spiritual home of San Francisco's Japanese-American population, even though comparatively few Japanese-Americans actually live here.

✚ H5 🚌 2, 3, 4, 22, 38

MISSION DISTRICT

With Latin American bakeries and restaurants, and some of its streets decorated by stunning murals (▶59), the Mission District holds the bulk of the city's Hispanic population. The neighborhood's Mexican-American population, established here in the 1940s, was joined from the 1970s by arrivals from Central America's war-torn countries.

✚ J/K 7/8/9 🚌 12, 14, 26, 33, 49, 67 🚇 16th Street Mission; 24th Street Mission

NOB HILL

A quartet of extremely wealthy Californians (the "Big Four," ▶12) built the first million-dollar mansions on Nob Hill from the 1870s. The 1906 earthquake and fire destroyed all but one of the district's opulent homes, but Nob Hill's place as a rich person's stamping ground is still evident. The area holds exclusive hotels and a very well-dressed congregation shows up for Sunday services at the neighborhood's Grace Cathedral (▶40).

✚ K5 🚌 1, 27; California Street cable car

Victorian houses near Russian Hill

NORTH BEACH

North Beach's wealth of cafés—serving top-quality coffee and a formidable array of cakes and pastries—and bookstores recall its links with the Beat Generation of the 1950s. Meanwhile, the abundant Italian-owned restaurants and stores are reminders of the Italians who settled the district in force from the late 19th century.

➕ K4 🚌 15, 30, 39, 41, 45, 83

PACIFIC HEIGHTS

Pacific Heights draws the wealthiest strata of San Franciscan society to its stately Victorian homes—some of them designed by architects who were attracted to California by the mid-19th-century Gold Rush—and high-rise luxury apartment buildings boasting wonderful views to Alcatraz and beyond.

➕ G/H/J 4/5 🚌 1, 3, 22, 24, 41, 42, 45, 47, 49

RUSSIAN HILL

A noted bohemian enclave in the late 19th century, Russian Hill is still a home of writers and artists, though only those with established reputations—and commensurate incomes—can afford to live among the successful doctors and lawyers who inhabit this quiet and cozy neighborhood today.

➕ J/K 3/4 🚌 41, 45; Powell–Hyde cable car

SOMA

Many of the former warehouses and factories of SoMa, an abbreviation of "South of Market Street," have been transformed into nightclubs, restaurants, and the offices of media companies. The biggest boost has been the development of the 12-block Yerba Buena Gardens cultural complex.

➕ J/K/L/M 5/6/7 🚌 10, 12, 14, 15, 20, 26, 27, 30, 45, 50, 60, 70, 76, 80

The Castro

The rainbow flags of gay solidarity are a common sight above the streets of the Castro, west of the Mission District, settled in large numbers by gay men (and by lesser numbers of lesbians) from the 1970s. As gays campaigned for and won a voice in city politics, the Castro evolved into the world's largest and most famous gay neighborhood.

51

PLACES OF WORSHIP

CHURCH OF SAINTS PETER AND PAUL

Long the major place of worship for North Beach's Italian community, this imposing Romanesque edifice was founded in 1922. The twin spires rise above Washington Square and are evocatively illuminated at night.

➕ K4 ✉ 666 Filbert Street ☎ 415/421 0809 🕐 Daily 7:30A.M.–8P.M. 🚋 15, 30, 39, 41, 45 ♿ Free

OLD ST. MARY'S CHURCH

The West Coast's first Catholic cathedral and a forerunner of today's ultramodern St. Mary's Cathedral (➤36), Old St. Mary's was completed in 1854.

➕ K5 ✉ 660 California Street ☎ 415/986 4388 🕐 Daily 6:30A.M.–5:30P.M . 🚋 1, 15; California Street cable car ♿ Free

ST. JOHN'S AFRICAN ORTHODOX CHURCH

Almost certainly the most curious church in San Francisco. See the panel for details.

➕ H7 ✉ 351 Divisadero Street ☎ 415/621 4054 🕐 Service Sun from 10A.M., Wed 6P.M. 🚋 24

SWEDENBORGIAN CHURCH

In keeping with Swedenborgian beliefs, this diminutive church resembles a finely crafted log cabin. Completed in 1895, the church was the work of several leading figures of the California Arts and Crafts movement.

➕ G5 ✉ 2107 Lyon Street ☎ 415/346 6466 🕐 Mon–Fri 9-5 🚋 3, 43 ♿ Free

TEMPLE EMANU-EL

This immense Byzantine-style structure, able to seat 2,000 people, looms above the surrounding residential architecture. Finished in 1926 at a cost of $3 million, the temple was raised to serve the longest-established Jewish congregation in California.

➕ F5 ✉ Lake Street and Arguello Boulevard ☎ 415/751 2535 🕐 Guided tours only: Mon–Fri 1-3 🚋 1, 4, 33, ♿ Free

TIEN HOU TEMPLE

Dating from 1852, this is the oldest and most atmospheric of Chinatown's incense-charged temples. Offerings of fruit, commonly oranges or tangerines, are placed before the altar by believers.

➕ K4 ✉ Fourth floor, 125 Waverly Place ☎ 415/391 4841 🕐 Erratic but usually Mon–Sat 10:30–4 🚋 1, 15, 30, 45, 83 ♿ Donation, inexpensive

Old St. Mary's Church

St. John's African Orthodox Church

St. John's African Orthodox Church, also known as "the Church of John Coltrane," was founded in 1971 by a jazz fan who underwent a religious experience when hearing saxophonist John Coltrane play live in the 1960s. The fan is now a sax-playing bishop who leads a congregation encouraged to bring instruments and to play them during the services.

MUSEUMS

A submarine tour

After touring the National Maritime Museum, continue the nautical theme by exploring the claustrophobic innards of USS *Pampanito*, moored a few minutes' walk away at Pier 45. Launched in 1943, the submarine saw action in the Pacific and sank 27,000 tons of enemy shipping. The cramped crews' and officers' quarters, the engine rooms, and the torpedo room are included on a self-guided tour.

CARTOON ART MUSEUM

Be they from comics, TV, or the movies—or culled from the deepest recesses of history—cartoons are accorded the seriousness of art in the changing exhibitions staged here, that seldom fail to be thought-provoking and entertaining.

🔲 L6 ✉ 814 Mission Street ☎ 415/546 3922 🕐 Wed–Fri 11–5; Sat 10–5; Sun 1–5 🚌 15, 30, 45 ♿ Moderate

NATIONAL MARITIME MUSEUM

A fine collection of figureheads, model ships, and other nautical memorabilia recall San Francisco's seafaring and shipbuilding past. The building itself resembles an ocean liner and provides a fine example of the 1930s art deco Streamline Moderne style.

🔲 J3 ✉ Aquatic Park, foot of Polk Street ☎ 415/556 3002 🕐 Daily 10A.M.–5P.M. 🚌 19, 32; Powell–Hyde cable car ♿ Free

NORTH BEACH MUSEUM

Temporary exhibitions of photos and paraphernalia document various episodes in the eventful past of this distinctive neighborhood.

🔲 K4 ✉ Mezzanine level, 1435 Stockton Street ☎ 415/391 6210 🕐 Mon–Thu 9-4; Fri 9–5 🚌 30, 45 ♿ Free

TATTOO ART MUSEUM

The posters, prints, and photographs lining the walls of this working tattoo parlor reveal some of the more extreme examples of the tattooist's art. Meanwhile a selection of gruesome tattooists' tools from times past suggest this form of body decoration has never been a popular option for the faint-hearted.

🔲 K4 ✉ 841 Columbus Avenue ☎ 415/775 4991 🕐 Usually 2P.M.–10P.M. 🚌 15, 30 ♿ Free

Moebius's "The Major," in the Cartoon Art Museum

MODERN BUILDINGS

> See Top 25 Sights for
> **ST. MARY'S CATHEDRAL ➤ 36**
> **SAN FRANCISCO MUSEUM OF**
> **MODERN ART ➤ 44**
> **TRANSAMERICA PYRAMID ➤ 45**

Art and architecture

Besides holding an excellent art collection, the San Francisco Museum of Modern Art (➤ 44) is also a distinguished architectural addition to the city. Opened in 1995, the $60-million museum was designed by Swiss architect Mario Botta, who gave it a stepped-back brick and stone façade. A truncated cylinder rising through the center allows light to flood the interior's full-height atrium.

The ultramodern architecture of the Rincon Center is complemented by this decorative stylus

BANK OF AMERICA HQ

No longer owned by the bank whose name it bears but still a supreme example of inspired 1960s high-rise office architecture. The 52-story building's dark red exterior, dominating the area by day, seems to become almost transparent at sunset.

➕ L5 ✉ 555 California Street 🚌 15, 42; California Street cable car

101 CALIFORNIA STREET

This Philip Johnson/John Burgee office tower is a soaring glass-sided silo that masquerades as a greenhouse at ground level.

➕ L5 ✉ 101 California Street 🚌 California Street cable car

CIRCLE GALLERY

During the late 1940s, architect Frank Lloyd Wright undertook a complete remodeling of this 1911 building and the design provided a foretaste of his acclaimed Guggenheim Museum in New York. The exterior brickwork is imbued with Mayan motifs; go inside to find the distinctive spiral ramp.

➕ K5 ✉ 140 Maiden Lane 🚌 2, 3, 4, 30, 45

GHIRARDELLI SQUARE

One of Fisherman's Wharf's successful conversions, the red-brick shell of the chocolate factory that opened here in 1893 now holds a strollable complex of stores and restaurants.

➕ J3 ✉ 900 North Point Street 🚌 19, 42; Powell–Hyde cable car

MARRIOTT HOTEL

A voluminous 40-story structure, the largest building in the city, the hotel sharply divided opinion when it opened in 1989. Newspaper columnist Herb Caen derisively dubbed it the "jukebox Marriott."

➕ L5 ✉ 777 Market Street 🚌 5, 6, 7, 8, 9, 21, 31, 38

RINCON CENTER

An office and shopping complex grafted with great style onto the rear of a 1930s art deco post office. The latter retains a vibrant 1939 mural depicting scenes from California's history.

➕ L/M5 ✉ Mission Street, between Spear and Steuart Streets 🚌 14

HISTORIC BUILDINGS

See Top 25 Sights for
MISSION DOLORES ▶ 34
NEPTUNE SOCIETY COLUMBARIUM ▶ 31
PALACE OF FINE ARTS ▶ 33

BANK OF CANTON
A three-tiered, pagoda-style structure erected in 1909 as the Chinatown telephone exchange, it was converted into a bank in the 1950s.
✚ K4 ✉ 743 Washington Street 🚌 1, 15, 30, 45

FERRY BUILDING
Completed in 1896, the 235-feet-high Ferry Building was for many years the city's tallest structure. Surviving the 1906 earthquake and fire—and a plan to demolish it for safety reasons during the disaster—the slender tower became a symbol of San Francisco's ability to survive natural catastrophe.
✚ M4 ✉ Foot of Market Street 🚌 5, 6, 7, 8, 9, 21, 31

HASS LILIENTHAL HOUSE
This elaborate 1886 example of the vertically-exaggerated "stick" style of architecture is also the only San Franciscan Victorian building to retain period-furnished rooms.
✚ J4 ✉ 2007 Franklin Street 🕐 Guided tours Wed 12–4; Sun 11–5 🚌 83 ♿ moderate

LEVI STRAUSS FACTORY
Built by Levi Strauss after the 1906 earthquake and still producing the world-famous jeans.
✚ J7 ✉ 250 Valencia Street ☎ 415/565 9153 🕐 Guided tours on selected dates by appointment 🚌 26

OCTAGON HOUSE
One of five eight-sided houses built in San Francisco, their shape considered lucky by the owners, the Octagon House dates from 1861. The restoration was organized by the Colonial Dames of America whose exhibitions of Colonial- and Federal-period arts and crafts now fill the interior.
✚ H4 ✉ 2645 Gough Street 🚌 41, 45

PACIFIC TELEPHONE BUILDING
A stylish skyscraper of the 1920s, its design heavily influenced by the work of Eliel Saarinen.
✚ L5 ✉ 140 New Montgomery Street 🚌 5, 6, 7, 8, 9, 15, 21, 30, 31, 38, 45, 71

VEDANTA TEMPLE
An extraordinary conglomeration of turquoise-colored towers, turrets, and domes, built in 1905 for an esoteric Eastern religious sect.
✚ H4 ✉ 2963 Webster Street 🚌 22, 41, 45

Octagon House

Levi's jeans

German-born entrepreneur Levi Strauss arrived in San Francisco in 1853 and began manufacture of what he called a "waist-high overall" for use by workers in the Californian gold mines. Hard-wearing, with tough seams, copper rivets, and numerous pockets, the Strauss garment evolved into "jeans" and their popularity spread across the American West and around the world.

55

GREEN SPACES

See Top 25 Sights for
GOLDEN GATE NATIONAL
RECREATION AREA ▶ 24
GOLDEN GATE PARK ▶ 25

Angel Island State Park

For a day in the wilds, make the short ferry crossing from Fisherman's Wharf to the mile-square Angel Island. The largest piece of land in San Francisco Bay, the island is a state park with foot trails and bike paths navigating its thickly forested heart. Also explorable are the remains of a military prison and of an immigration processing center.

HUNTINGTON PARK

Facing Grace Cathedral (▶ 40), Huntington Park occupies the plot of an 1872 mansion and is named after one of the "Big Four" railroad barons (▶ 12).
➕ K5 ✉ Bordered by California, Sacramento, Taylor, and Cushman Streets 🚋 1; California Street cable car

INA COOLBRITH PARK

A tiny but abundantly vegetated park accessed by steps and named for the woman who, in 1919, became California's first poet laureate. Coolbrith's literary get-togethers, held at her Russian Hill home, were legendary.
➕ K4 ✉ Bordered by Taylor and Vallejo Streets 🚋 Powel—Mason cable car

LAFAYETTE PARK

The highest point in Pacific Heights and overlooked by the splendid Spreckels Mansion, completed in 1912 as the home of sugar-baron Adolph Spreckels and his wife.
➕ H/J 5 ✉ Bordered by Gough, Laguna, Sacramento, and Washington Streets 🚋 1, 12

Washington Square,
North Beach

MARINA GREEN

Kite-flying, jogging, and the walking of well-bred dogs are among the popular pursuits in this bay-side green strip, overlooked by pastel-colored stucco-fronted houses and serving an affluent neighborhood.
➕ G/H 3 ✉ Beside Marina Boulevard 🚋 22

TRANSAMERICA REDWOOD PARK

Located behind the Transamerica Pyramid (▶ 45) and a welcome break from the hubbub of the Financial District, this slender park holds young redwood trees and stages free lunchtime concerts on weekdays.
➕ L4 ✉ Bordered by Washington and Clay Streets 🚋 15, 41

WASHINGTON SQUARE

Packed each morning with Chinese going through their Tai Chi routines, this North Beach park is also the scene for enjoyable art shows each weekend.
➕ K4 ✉ Bordered by Columbus Avenue, Filbert, Union, and Stockton Streets 🚋 15, 30, 39, 41, 45

VIEWS

See Top 25 Sights for
**CALIFORNIA PALACE OF THE LEGION OF
    HONOR ►26
TRANSAMERICA PYRAMID ►45**

ALAMO SQUARE
Perhaps the most-photographed view in San
Francisco finds the six Victorian homes, or "painted
ladies," on the east side of Alamo Square contrasting
with the modern towers of the Financial District
visible in the background.
➕ H6 ✉ Bordered by Hayes, Fulton, Scott, and Steiner Streets
🚌 21

COIT TOWER
Whether from the top of the tower or from its base,
the outlook across San Francisco Bay and a huge
swath of the city is a memorable one.
➕ K3 ✉ Summit of Telegraph Hill Boulevard 🚌 39

FAIRMONT HOTEL CROWN ROOM ELEVATOR
The glass-sided elevator that rises nonstop from
ground-level to the 22nd-floor Crown Room
restaurant brings vertiginous views of the Financial
District as it recedes far below.
➕ K5 ✉ 950 Mason Street 🚋 1; California Street cable car

SUTRO HEIGHTS PARK
From the former grounds of the home of legendary
19th-century San Francisco benefactor Adolph Sutro
are fabulous views of the city's Pacific coast and the
western end of Golden Gate Park. Remnants of
the house and its statuary are scattered about the
park's footpaths.
➕ A6 ✉ Bordered by Point Lobos Avenue, Great Highway, and
48th Street 🚌 18, 38

TWIN PEAKS
One of the best overall views of San Francisco comes,
not surprisingly, from one of its highest points, the
913-feet summit of the two hills known as Twin Peaks;
even on foot, the exhausting ascent is worthwhile.
➕ G9 ✉ Summit of Twin Peaks Boulevard 🚌 37

*The view from
Twin Peaks*

Coit Tower's murals

The external view is one reason
for visiting Coit Tower, another is
the excellent murals lining the
interior walls. Painted as part of
a Depression-era project to give
work to artists, the left-wing
political content of the murals—
by several artists and showing
Californian scenes—caused great
controversy during the early
1930s and delayed the tower's
official opening.

ATTRACTIONS FOR CHILDREN

BEACHES

China and Baker beaches (part of Golden Gate National Recreation Area, ➤24) make appealing locations for enjoying a picnic and a frolic in the sand. The sea lions of Seal Rocks might provide sufficient incentive for embarking on the scenically dramatic coastal trail.

Few can resist a ride on a cable car

CABLE CAR RIDE

Any cable car is an enjoyable adventure for most children, but to avoid the lines at the main embarkation points take the California Street line, which includes a dramatic climb to (and descent from) Nob Hill.
✉ Operate on three routes (➤90). ☎ General public transport information 415/673 MUNI ⏰ Hours of operation 6A.M.–1A.M. 🎫 Inexpensive

Pier 39's sea lions

Introducing young minds to the wonders of natural California can easily be accomplished at Fisherman's Wharf's Pier 39. Attracted by an abundant supply of herring, some 600 California sea lions have made their homes beside the pier and can be observed from a marked viewing area. A naturalist arrives to talk about the creatures most weekend afternoons (details: ☎ 415/289 7325).

JOSEPHINE S. RANDALL JUNIOR MUSEUM

A zoo with animals to pet and a nature walk are the main attractions, but there are also science exhibits—such as a mineral collection and a seismograph—to entertain and inform young minds.
➕ H8 ✉ 199 Museum Way ☎ 415/554 9600 ⏰ Tue–Sun 10–5 🚌 37 🎫 Free

RIPLEY'S BELIEVE IT OR NOT!

An eight-foot-long cable car made from 275,000 matchsticks, a display about the man who could whistle while holding three golf balls in his mouth, and a room devoted to a simulated Californian earthquake are among the mass of strangely compelling delights that children are likely to relish.
➕ K3 ✉ 175 Jefferson Street ☎ 415/771 6188 ⏰ Sun–Thu 9A.M.–11P.M.; Fri and Sat 9A.M.–midnight 🚌 15, 30, 32, 39, 42; Powell–Mason cable car 🎫 Moderate

SAN FRANCISCO ZOOLOGICAL GARDENS

Awkwardly located on the fringes of the city, this zoo nevertheless holds the usual complement of creatures, plus a state-of-the-art primate center and a Children's Zoo where furry creatures aplenty await a stroking.
➕ Off map ✉ Sloat Boulevard and 45th Avenue ☎ 415/753 7080; recorded information 415/753 7083 ⏰ Daily 10–5 🚌 18, 23; L 🎫 Moderate; free first Wed of each month

FREE ATTRACTIONS

DIEGO RIVERA GALLERY

An immense mural by the Mexican master, Diego Rivera, sits at one end of this gallery of the highly respected San Francisco Institute of Art, while student works line the other three walls.

✚ J3 ⊠ 800 Chestnut Street ☎ 415/749 4567 ⏱ Mon–Fri 9–5
🚌 15, 30, 41; Powell–Hyde cable car

FIRE DEPARTMENT MUSEUM

Fires were frequent occurrences in early San Francisco and firefighting quickly became a job of paramount importance. In this small but copiously filled room, buckets, hoses, helmets, and other intriguing firefighting trivia form a huge and entertaining clutter.

✚ G5 ⊠ 655 Presidio Avenue ☎ 415/861 8000
⏱ Thu–Sun 1–4 🚌 43

FORT POINT NATIONAL HISTORIC SITE

Completed in 1861, Fort Point was intended to deter enemy incursions into San Francisco Bay but never a shot was fired in anger. Period-attired guides describe the fort's past, while temporary indoor exhibitions explore diverse aspects of U.S. military history.

✚ D3 ⊠ Beneath Golden Gate Bridge ☎ 415/556 1693
⏱ Wed–Sun 10–5 🚌 28, 29, 76

MISSION DISTRICT MURALS

Some of the best of the Mission District's many murals, reflecting Latin American muralist traditions, line this alley and focus on a theme of peace in Central America. Visit during daylight hours.

✚ K9 ⊠ Balmy Alley, between 24th and 25th Streets
☎ 415/285 2287 (Precita Eyes Mural Center) 🚌 12, 27, 67

TELEPHONE PIONEER COMMUNICATIONS MUSEUM

Located on the ground floor of the eye-catching Pacific Telephone Building (▶55), this museum documents Californian communications past, present, and future, with displays on everything from ancient switchboards to the latest satellite technology.

✚ L5 ⊠ 140 New Montgomery Street ☎ 415/542 0182
⏱ Mon–Fri 10–3 🚌 5, 6, 7, 8, 9, 15, 21, 30, 31, 38, 45, 71

Hotel art

Public areas in San Franciscan hotels can prove rewarding for art and photography enthusiasts: the Sheraton Palace (▶ 84) has an excellent Maxfield Parrish mural; Gustav Klimt prints line the Redwood Room at the Four Seasons Clift (▶ 81); and the Compass Rose Room at the Westin St. Francis (▶ 84) holds photographs by Ansel Adams.

Firefighting relics in the Fire Department Museum

INTRIGUING STREETS

GREEN STREET

Among the numerous architecturally distinguished survivors of the 1906 earthquake and fire along this single block are the Feusier Octagon House, number 1067, one of the city's two remaining eight-sided homes (▶55).

✚ J/K 4 ✉ Between Jones and Leavenworth Streets 🚌 41, 45; Powell–Hyde cable car

LOMBARD STREET

Traffic zigzags down Lombard Street at five miles per hour, moving around colorful gardens put in place during the 1920s.

✚ J4 ✉ Between Hyde and Leavenworth Streets 🚌 15, 19, 30

MACONDRAY LANE

With leafy trees shading its cottages, most of which were raised in the construction boom that followed the 1906 earthquake, pedestrianized Macondray Lane is the epitome of quaint and cozy Russian Hill.

✚ J/K 4 ✉ Between Taylor and Leavenworth Streets 🚌 41, 45; Powell–Hyde cable car

MAIDEN LANE

Notorious for its brothels in the 1800s, Maiden Lane is now lined by upscale shops and bordered by fancy wooden gates.

✚ K/L5 ✉ Between Stockton and Kearny Streets 🚌 2, 3, 4, 30, 45

UNION STREET

The affluent and fashionable residents of Pacific Heights shop, eat, and socialize along these few chic blocks.

✚ H/J4 ✉ Between Franklin and Steiner Streets 🚌 22, 41, 45

VALENCIA STREET

A Mission District thoroughfare known for its smattering of feminist- and women's-interest shops and cafés amid anonymous warehouses and car-repair workshops.

✚ J 8/9 ✉ Between 16th and 24th Streets 🚌 26

WAVERLY PLACE

A Chinatown side street holding three temples, numerous Chinese family association buildings, and the decorations that earn it the name "street of painted balconies."

✚ K 4/5 ✉ Between Sacramento and Washington Streets 🚌 1, 15, 30, 45, 83

Filbert Steps

Steep gradients are a San Franciscan specialty and often cause streets to become flights of steps. One such is the Filbert Steps, running between Telegraph Hill (from Coit Tower) and Levi's Plaza. Curiously, the gardens that line Filbert Steps are the result of the horticultural enterprise of a one-time Hollywood stunt lady, who moved here on her retirement in 1949.

SAN FRANCISCO
where to...

EXPENSIVE RESTAURANTS

Prices

Average meal per head
excluding drink

$ = up to $15

$$ = up to $30

$$$ = over $30

Except for the luxury restaurants
on this page, where dinner will
easily cost upwards of $60
excluding wine for two people
(lunch will be less; typically
around $40), dining in San
Francisco is a cost-effective
experience. Anticipate spending
$6–$8 per person for breakfast,
around $10 for lunch, and
$15–$20 for dinner excluding
drinks. Wherever you dine, a tip
of at least 15 per cent of the
total is expected; reward
extremely good service with a tip
of 20 per cent or more.

Opening times

Peak hours for lunch are
11:30–2, and for dinner
5:30–9, but many restaurants
open earlier and/or close later
than these times.

ACT IV ($$$)

Californian cuisine
with a Mediterranean
slant; a favorite haunt of
visiting opera and
theater stars.

➕ J6 ✉ Inn at the Opera
Hotel, 333 Fulton Street
☎ 415/863 8400 🕐 No lunch
on weekends 🚌 5, 21

AQUA ($$$)

Carefully prepared and
presented seafood draws
a style-conscious crowd
to this modernistic
eaterie.

➕ L4 ✉ 252 California Street
☎ 415/956 9662 🚌 1, 41;
California Street cable car

CAFÉ MAJESTIC ($$$)

Inventive Californian
dishes with a European
twist; the Edwardian
dining room is regularly
heralded as San
Francisco's most
romantic dining spot.

➕ J5 ✉ 1500 Sutter Street
☎ 415/776 6400 🕐 No lunch
weekends or Mon 🚌 2, 4

CAMPTON PLACE ($$$)

The ever-changing
menu reflects the fact
that only the freshest
local produce is used to
create dishes especially
valued for their natural
flavors.

➕ K5 ✉ Campton Place Hotel,
340 Stockton Street
☎ 415/955 5555 🚌 30, 45

FLEUR DE LYS ($$$)

More formal than
many, jacket and tie
required, and serving
San Francisco's best
French food.

➕ K5 ✉ 777 Sutter Street
☎ 415/673 7779 🕐 Dinner
only 🚌 2, 3, 4, 7

MASA'S ($$$)

A very fine Californian-
French restaurant
renowned for its quality.
Usually booked weeks
in advance, although
cancellations can make
tables available at
short notice.

➕ K5 ✉ Vintage Court Hotel,
648 Bush Street ☎ 415/989
7154 🕐 Dinner only; closed
Sun, Mon 🚌 2, 3, 4, 30, 76

POSTRIO ($$$)

Run by celebrity chef
Wolfgang Puck and the
epitome of California-
style gourmet dining,
utilizing fresh local
produce.

➕ K5 ✉ 545 Post Street
☎ 415/776 7825
🚌 2, 3, 4, 76

SILKS ($$$)

A blend of contemporary
American cuisine and
Asian subtlety in an
elegant setting.

➕ L5 ✉ Mandarin Oriental
Hotel, 222 Sansome Street
☎ 415/986 2020 🚌 42

STARS ($$$)

Hot spot for socialites
and gossip columnists;
varied fare but usually
strongest on seafood.

➕ J6 ✉ 150 Redwood Street
☎ 415/861 7827
🕐 No lunch on weekends
🚌 5, 42, 47, 49

TOMMY TOY'S ($$$)

French and Chinese
influences combine in
an imaginative menu;
the setting is an opulent
one and the service is
famously attentive.

➕ L4 ✉ 655 Montgomery
Street ☎ 415/397 4888
🚌 15, 41 🕐 No lunch
on weekends

BUDGET RESTAURANTS

ART INSTITUTE CAFÉ ($)

Simple pasta dishes and assorted snacks can be consumed with a splendid view across the local rooftops to San Francisco Bay; part of San Francisco Art Institute.

✚ J3　✉ 800 Chestnut Street　☎ 415/749 4567　🕐 Lunch　🚌 15, 30, 41; Powell–Hyde cable car

CARAVANSARY ($)

A promising array of Middle Eastern delights is offered alongside the usual American diner fare.

✚ G4　✉ 2257 Chestnut Street　☎ 415/922 2705　🕐 Lunch and early dinner　🚌 30

DOTTIE'S TRUE BLUE CAFÉ ($)

Small, friendly diner with great start-the-day omelets and a variety of health-conscious lunches.

✚ K5　✉ 522 Jones Street　☎ 415/885 2767　🕐 Breakfast and lunch　🚌 27

EAGLE CAFÉ ($)

Serving well-filled omelets and substantial sandwiches since the 1920s and providing an authentic slice of local life in a touristy area; order at the counter and wait for your number to be called.

✚ K3　✉ Pier 39　☎ 415/433 3689　🕐 Breakfast and lunch　🚌 32

EL TORO TAQUERIA ($)

Burritos in many varieties and other low-cost, well-prepared Mexican favorites are the stock-in-trade of this busy eaterie in the strongly Hispanic Mission District.

✚ J8　✉ 598 Valencia Street　☎ 415/431 3351　🚌 26

HAMBURGER MARY'S ORGANIC GRILL ($)

Garishly decorated and often patronized by a nightclubbing clientele, Mary's offers specialist burgers as well as a tempting selection of soups, sandwiches, and salads.

✚ K7　✉ 1582 Folsom Street　☎ 415/626 5767　🚌 12

NEW DAWN ($)

Combines crazy decor and an anything-goes ambience with large helpings of no-nonsense American cooking.

✚ J8　✉ 3174 16th Street　☎ 415/553 8888　🕐 Breakfast and lunch　🚌 22

NORTH BEACH PIZZA ($)

The thick, chewy pizzas served with a host of toppings are famous throughout the city and often result in a line forming outside in the evenings; a newer branch is down the hill at 1310 Grant Avenue.

✚ K4　✉ 1499 Grant Avenue　☎ 415/433 2444　🕐 Lunch and dinner　🚌 15, 30, 41, 45

PAG ASA KITCHEN EXPRESS ($)

Filipino fare served cafeteria style; very popular but in an unsalubrious area.

✚ K6　✉ 350 Golden Gate Avenue　☎ 415/776 8082　🕐 Breakfast and lunch　🚌 31

Eating with children

All but the most exclusive San Franciscan restaurants welcome children. Young diners will often be handed toys and coloring sets as soon as they sit down, and they have their own section of the menu, where child-sized portions and perennial kids' favorites such as burgers and French fries are strongly featured.

CHINESE RESTAURANTS

Dim sum

Popular at lunchtime, *dim sum* consists of various small dishes offered to diners from carts. The cost is determined by the number of empty dishes on your table. Favorite dim sum dishes include *Cha Sil Bow*—steamed pork bun; *Gai Bow*—steamed chicken bun; *Chern Goon*—spring rolls; *Sil Mi*—steamed pork and shrimp dumpling. Less popular ones among Westerners include *Gai Guerk*—braised chicken feet, and *Op Guerk*—braised duck's feet.

BRANDY HO'S ($$)
Earning deserved acclaim for its Hunan cuisine; diners with delicate palates might find some of the spicier dishes too hot to handle.

✚ K/L4   ✉ 450-2 Broadway
☎ 415/362 6268
🚌 15, 30, 45, 83

CHINA HOUSE BISTRO ($$)
The regional cuisines of northern China, including many Shanghai specialties, created with typical Californian flair.

✚ E6   ✉ 501 Balboa Street
☎ 415/752 2802   🕙 Dinner only   🚌 31

HONG KONG FLOWER LOUNGE ($$)
Some of the best Cantonese fare in San Francisco and top-notch *dim sum* at lunchtime.

✚ D6   ✉ 5322 Geary Boulevard   ☎ 415/668 8998
🚌 38

HOUSE OF NANKING ($)
Tiny, well-regarded restaurant which was among the first to bring quality Shanghai and northern regional Chinese cooking to San Francisco.

✚ K4   ✉ 919 Kearny Street
☎ 415/421 1429   🚌 15

KOWLOON VEGETARIAN RESTAURANT ($)
Meal-in-themselves soups, and assorted rice and noodle dishes make up the 89-item menu.

✚ K4   ✉ 909 Grant Avenue
☎ 415/362 9888
🚌 1, 15, 30, 45, 83

LOTUS GARDEN ($$)
Vegetarian Chinese fare in a more upscale setting than the Kowloon (see above) and with greater culinary creativity shown.

✚ K5   ✉ 532 Grant Avenue
☎ 415/397 0707
🚌 1, 15, 30, 45

POT STICKER ($)
Located in a temple-laden Chinatown side-street, the restaurant specializes in steamed and pan-fried dumplings filled with meat, seafood, or vegetables.

✚ K4   ✉ 150 Waverly Place
☎ 415/397 9985
🚌 1, 15, 30, 45

ROYAL JADE ($/$$)
Cantonese seafood is the house speciality, though excellent *dim sum* is served at lunchtime when there is also a low cost buffet offered on the top floor.

✚ K4   ✉ 675 Jackson Street
☎ 415/392 2929   🚌 1, 15, 30, 45, 83

WU KONG ($$$)
The Shanghai cuisine on offer here will appease the most demanding gourmet.

✚ L/M4   ✉ Rincon Center, 101 Spear Street   ☎ 415/957 9300   🚌 1, 14, 32

YANK SING ($$)
Just outside Chinatown in the Financial District and pricier than some, this restaurant is one of the best local lunch stops on account of its *dim sum*.

✚ L4   ✉ 427 Battery Street
☎ 415/362 1640
🕙 Lunch only   🚌 42

ITALIAN RESTAURANTS

BASTA PASTA ($$)
Fine pastas and succulent wood-fired pizzas provide the main appeal, although the large windows are a bonus.
✚ K4 ✉ 1268 Grant Avenue ☎ 415/434 2248 🚌 15, 30, 41, 45

BUCA GIOVANNI ($$/$$$)
Not many visitors stumble on this basement restaurant that serves some of the best Tuscan-style food around.
✚ K4 ✉ 800 Greenwich Street ☎ 415/776 7766 🕐 Dinner only 🚌 15, 30, 41, 45

CAFÉ ROCCO ($$)
Good selection of northern Italian fare and a delightful patio on which to eat it.
✚ K6 ✉ 1131 Folsom Street ☎ 415/554 0522 🚌 12

CAPP'S CORNER ($/$$)
Owned by a former boxing champion, Capp's has delicious pasta lunches and serves five-course set dinners, as well as a full menu.
✚ K4 ✉ 1600 Powell Street ☎ 415/989 2589 🕐 No lunch on weekends 🚌 15, 30, 41, 45

FIOR D'ITALIA ($$$)
Among San Francisco's oldest and best Italian restaurants with wonderfully fresh pasta dishes served either in the elegant backroom or overlooking Washington Square.
✚ K4 ✉ 601 Union Street ☎ 415/986 1886 🚌 15, 30, 41, 45

GOLD SPIKE ($)
Filled to bursting point almost every night for unbeatable North Beach atmosphere and six-course dinners.
✚ K4 ✉ 527 Columbus Avenue ☎ 415/421 4591 🚌 15, 30, 41, 45

THE NEW SAN REMO RESTAURANT ($)
Its location, a few minutes' walk from the busiest North Beach streets, helps this quiet northern Italian restaurant keep down the cost of its five-course dinners.
✚ K3 ✉ 2237 Mason Street ☎ 415/673 9090 🚌 15, 30, 39, 41

NORTH BEACH RESTAURANT ($$$)
Among North Beach's more elegant and formal Italian restaurants, the choices include a fixed price seven-course dinner.
✚ K4 ✉ 1512 Stockton Street ☎ 415/392 1700 🚌 15, 30, 41, 45

TOMMASO'S ($$)
Delicious pizza and *calzone* served in an intimate room make this one of North Beach's most popular dining spots.
✚ K4 ✉ 1042 Kearny Street ☎ 415/398 9696 🚌 15, 30, 41, 45, 83

VIVA'S ($)
Tremendous northern Italian specialties and some excellent seafood dishes.
✚ K4 ✉ 1224 Grant Avenue ☎ 415/989 8482 🚌 15, 41, 83

Seafood specials
During its mid-November to June season, the creamy and chewy Dungeness crab becomes a feature of many San Franciscan menus. Many Italian restaurants serve it as the centerpiece of a Italian-San Franciscan seafood dish called *cioppino*, a throw-everything-in type of fish stew that, the story goes, was first concocted by the wives of the city's late-1800s Sicilian settlers. Dungeness crab also claws its way onto menus elsewhere. In Chinatown, look for it deliciously prepared in ginger and garlic.

INDIAN & VEGETARIAN RESTAURANTS

INDIAN

APPAM, CUISINE OF OLD INDIA ($$)

Uses the traditional Dum Pakht method of cooking dishes in a sealed clay pot.

✚ K7 ✉ 1259 Folsom Street
☎ 415/626 2798 🚌 12, 76

GAYLORD INDIA RESTAURANT ($$)

In an attractive location with striking views across the Golden Gate, Gaylord specializes in northern Indian fare.

✚ J3 ✉ Ghirardelli Square, 900 North Point Street
☎ 415/771 8822 🚌 19, 42

NORTH INDIA ($$)

The setting adds to the atmosphere and the hotter dishes carry a touch more spiciness than most Indian restaurants.

✚ H4 ✉ 3131 Webster Street
☎ 415/931 1556
🚌 22, 41, 46

SCENIC INDIA ($)

This restaurant offers a slightly predictable but well-priced and satisfying selection of curries and tandoori dishes.

✚ J8 ✉ 532 Valencia Street
☎ 415/621 7226 🚌 26

SIRTAJ ($)

The 13-course lunch buffet is a cost-effective way to sample Indian fare. Also features good-value set dinners.

✚ K6 ✉ 48 Fifth Street
☎ 415/957 0140 🚌 27
Ⓜ Powell Street

STAR OF INDIA ($)

Many mouthwatering vegetarian selections help to make this low-key spot one of San Francisco's more appealing Indian eateries; the weekday lunch buffet is exceptional value.

✚ F6 ✉ 3721 Geary Boulevard ☎ 415/668 4466
🚌 38

VEGETARIAN

ANANDA FUARA ($)

A serene atmosphere prevails at this vegetarian restaurant, run by an (unobtrusive) religious sect, where "meatloaf" served with gravy and potatoes is one popular option.

✚ J6 ✉ 1298 Market Street
☎ 415/621 1994 🚌 6, 7, 66, 71 Ⓜ Van Ness

COUNTER CULTURE CAFÉ ($)

Good selection of meat free light meals and snacks.

✚ J7 ✉ 2073 Market Street
☎ 415/621 7488 🚌 37

GREENS ($$$)

An outstanding vegetarian restaurant where gourmet-pleasing dishes are created using the produce of an organic farm run at a Zen Buddhist retreat on the north side of San Francisco Bay. The bay views are as stunning as the food, and reservations are essential.

✚ H3 ✉ Building A, Fort Mason Center ☎ 415/771 6222 🚌 22, 28, 30, 47, 49

VEGI FOOD ($)

Intriguing and inviting vegetarian dishes are on offer here, mostly based on Chinese cuisine.

✚ D6 ✉ 1820 Clement Street ☎ 415/387 8111
🚌 2

Sourdough bread

The slightly bitter and chewy sourdough bread served in many San Franciscan restaurants first appeared here during the Gold Rush (and was first baked commercially by a French San Franciscan settler called Isadore Boudin). Yeast and baking powder were scarce and settlers made bread using a sour starter, a fermented mixture of flour and water that enabled the dough to rise. San Franciscan folklore holds that the quality of a sourdough loaf is dependent upon the local fog.

JAPANESE & SOUTHEAST ASIAN RESTAURANTS

JAPANESE

ISOBUNE ($$)

Watch the chef prepare *sushi*, then make your selection from the many little *sushi*-laden boats that float along the counter.

H5 Japan Center, Japantown 415/563 1030
2, 3, 4, 22, 38

KYO-YA ($$$)

In keeping with the luxurious ambience of this elegant hotel, Kyo-Ya serves the finest Japanese food in San Francisco; reservations are recommended.

L5 Sheraton Palace Hotel, 2 New Montgomery Street 415/392 8600 Closed on weekends 5, 6, 7, 8, 9, 21, 31, 38, 42, 45, 71
Montgomery Street

SOUTHEAST ASIAN

ANGKOR PALACE ($$)

There are less costly places to enjoy high-quality Cambodian food in San Francisco, but this is one of the few where diners remove their shoes on entering and are seated on floor cushions.

H4 1769 Lombard Street 415/931 2830
43, 76

PHEU ANG THAI ($$)

This restaurant offers an extensive menu of Thai soups, salads, and curry dishes; the noodle and rice dishes are generally particularly good value.

H4 2001 Union Street 415/775 4735 41, 45

SAIGON SAIGON ($$)

Black pepper catfish and coconut chicken are among the specialties of this highly rated and fairly priced Vietnamese eaterie.

J9 1132 Valencia Street 415/206 9635 26

SORNDANG CAFÉ ($)

A cheap and cheerful place in which to enjoy a good-value Thai lunch or dinner, though the neighborhood can seem intimidating.

J/K6 472 Turk Street 415/474 8377 19, 31

STRAITS CAFÉ ($$)

Offers a range of dishes that mix and match various Southeast Asian cuisines; many vegetarian options and a strong choice of seafood dishes.

F6 3300 Geary Boulevard 415/668 1783
38

THAI SPICE ($)

First class Thai food served in an airy setting puts this among the city's premier ethnic eating spots; an enormous menu includes an impressive number of vegetarian dishes.

J5 1730 Polk Street 415/775 4777 19

THAI STICK ($$)

Good quality, centrally located Thai with all the usual favorites plus a number of house specialties, including a delicious tapioca pudding dessert.

K5 698 Post Street 415/928 7730
2, 3, 4, 76

Brunch

Brunch is a Sunday social fixture for many San Franciscans. Costing $8-$20, depending on the restaurant serving it and the combination of food and alcohol that is included in the price, brunch usually lasts from 10A.M. to 2P.M. The restaurant sections of local newspapers and magazines have plenty of suggestions on what are the best brunch spots. Be sure to make a reservation before turning up.

CAFÉS

Coffee San Francisco-style

San Franciscans place great importance on the quality of coffee. Cafés listed here are chosen for their food (for those suited to evening socializing ►82), but most also pride themselves on the excellence of their coffee beans and serve the drink in several main forms. Besides *espresso* (coffee brewed at high pressure) and *cappuccino* (espresso topped by a creamy milk head), coffee is commonly served as *caffè latté* (espresso with steamed milk) and *caffè mocha* (espresso with chocolate).

BRAIN WASH ($)
A truly San Franciscan phenomenon: a café attached to a launderette enabling patrons to drink coffee and munch cakes while their washing is being done.
✚ K6 ✉ 1122 Folsom Street ☎ 415/861 3663 🚌 12

BUENA VISTA CAFÉ ($)
A good bet for simple, inexpensive food in a pricey area, though best known for its punch-packing Irish coffee.
✚ J3 ✉ 2765 Hyde Street ☎ 415/474 5044 🚌 32

CAFÉ BASTILLE ($)
A very effective re-creation of a stylish Parisian bistro in a Financial District alley.
✚ L5 ✉ 22 Belden Alley ☎ 415/986 5673 🚌 15

CAFÉ ISTANBUL ($)
Offers extra-strong Turkish coffee and a delicious selection of very sweet cakes and pastries.
✚ J8 ✉ 525 Valencia Street ☎ 415/863 8854 🚌 26 🚇 16th Street Mission

CAFÉ LA BOHÈME ($)
San Francisco's present-day Bohemia in the Mission District is well-served by this roomy outlet for coffee, soups and snacks—and pickup chess games.
✚ J9 ✉ 3318 24th Street ☎ 415/285 4122 🚌 14, 26, 48, 67 🚇 BART 24th Street Mission

CAFFÈ TRIESTE ($)
Since it opened in the 1950s, Trieste has been the quintessential North Beach café, drawing writers, poets, artists, and anyone seeking a flavorful cup of coffee and a choice of tempting cakes and snacks; amateur operatic performances are staged here on Saturday afternoons.
✚ K4 ✉ 601 Vallejo Street ☎ 415/392 6739 🚌 15, 41

JAMMIN' JAVA ($)
A perfect place to begin exploring Haight-Ashbury; counter-cultural artworks are displayed alongside wholesome snacks and excellent coffee.
✚ F7 ✉ 701 Cole Street ☎ 415/668 5282 🚌 37

JUST DESSERTS ($)
One of a small San Franciscan café chain, this branch is located usefully close to Fort Mason Center (►35).
✚ H3 ✉ 3735 Buchanan Street ☎ 415/922 8675 🚌 28

KAN ZAMAN ($)
An inspired addition to the city's café scene: the deep cushions, large hookahs and selection of Arabian snacks are memorable.
✚ F7 ✉ 1793 Haight Street ☎ 415/751 9656 🚌 6, 7, 33, 43, 66, 71

MARIO'S BOHEMIAN CIGAR STORE ($)
Another long-established North Beach café that offers excellent *focaccia* bread snacks.
✚ K4 ✉ 566 Columbus Avenue ☎ 415/362 0536 🚌 15, 30, 41, 45

AFTERNOON TEAROOMS

ACORN TEA & GRIDDLE ($/$$)
A rare opportunity for afternoon tea in the SoMa neighborhood.
K7 ✉ 1256 Folsom Street ☎ 415/863 2469 🚌 12

BREAD & HONEY TEAROOM ($)
Tea and nibbles are served with minimal fuss in a simple setting.
K5 ✉ King George Hotel, 334 Mason Street ☎ 415/781 5050 🚌 2, 3, 4, 38, 76

COMPASS ROSE ($$)
San Francisco's high society lines up for the privilege of enjoying a tempting selection of teas and the most delicate of sandwiches in this luxurious room.
K5 ✉ Westin St. Francis Hotel, 335 Powell Street at Union Square ☎ 415/774 0167 🚌 2, 3, 4, 6, 38, 71; Powell–Hyde and Powell–Mason cable cars

FOUR SEASONS CLIFT HOTEL ($$)
A decent spread, but unfortunately served in an undistinguished corner of the lobby rather than in one of the hotel's more famous public rooms.
K5 ✉ 495 Geary Street ☎ 415/775 4700 🚌 38

GARDEN COURT ($$)
Afternoon tea is offered in the Garden Court, the city's most ornate interior, to the accompaniment of a harpist.
L5 ✉ Sheraton Palace Hotel, 2 New Montgomery Street ☎ 415/392 8600 🚌 5, 6, 7, 8, 9, 21, 31, 38, 42, 45, 71 Ⓜ Montgomery Street

LOWER BAR ($$)
Afternoon tea is a good excuse for sampling this hotel's legendary farmhouse fruitcake.
K5 ✉ Mark Hopkins Intercontinental Hotel, 1 Nob Hill ☎ 415/392 3434 🚌 1; California Street cable car

MAD MAGDA'S RUSSIAN TEA ROOM ($)
A contrast to the refinement elsewhere, Magda's brings avant-garde décor and general eccentricity to the consumption of tea and scones.
J6 ✉ 579 Hayes Street ☎ 415/864 7654 🚌 21

NEIMAN MARCUS ROTUNDA ($$)
Tea beneath this store's immense rotunda, dating from 1909, includes a bird's-eye view of Union Square.
K5 ✉ Neiman Marcus, 150 Stockton Street ☎ 415/362 3900 🚌 38; Powell–Hyde or Powell–Mason cable car

RITZ-CARLTON ($$)
A good choice of teas, sandwiches, and feather-light cakes; the sense of decadent pleasure is heightened by a pianist.
K5 ✉ 600 Stockton Street ☎ 415/296 7465 🚌 1, 30, 45; California Street cable car

STANFORD COURT HOTEL ($$)
Served in the hushed surroundings of the lobby lounge, the tea spread includes smoked salmon with *crème fraîche* on pumpernickel.
K5 ✉ 905 California Street ☎ 415/989 3500 🚌 1; California Street cable car

The complete tea
Afternoon tea costs around $20 and typically offers a choice of Earl Grey, orange pekoe, Darjeeling, jasmine, lapsang souchong, oolong, peppermint, Russian caravan, or chamomile tea. This will be served with any or all of the following: sandwiches (filled with bacon, cucumber, smoked salmon, ham, egg and parsley, or English cheddar cheese), scones, and fancy pastries. Devonshire cream and assorted fine jams await application to your scone, but the first item to be eaten should be the palate-cleansing cucumber sandwiches.

DEPARTMENT STORES & SHOPPING CENTERS

Neiman Marcus's architecture

Neiman Marcus's 1982 opening was met with a certain sadness by San Franciscans who, whatever their feelings for the store itself, were generally not enamored of its austere Post-Modern design (from architects Philip Johnson and John Burgee) or the fact that it replaced the City of Paris department store building that had occupied the site since 1896. The latter's immense glass rotunda was retained, however, and can best be admired over afternoon tea in the Rotunda restaurant (➤69).

CROCKER GALLERIA

Designer clothing stores, food shops, and snack stands make this small, chic shopping mall in the Financial District ideal for idle browsing.
➕ L5 ✉ 50 Post Street
☎ 415/393 1505
🚋 2, 3, 4, 5, 6

EMBARCADERO CENTER

A three-level shopping complex spanning eight city blocks; pick up a free map to plot a course around the walkways, plazas, and scores of interesting stores.
➕ L4 ✉ Battery Street, between Clay and Sacramento Streets ☎ 415/772 0500
🚋 1, 41, 42

GHIRARDELLI SQUARE

A chocolate factory thoughtfully converted to house a range of entertaining stores, all with merchandise a cut above the standard tourist items found elsewhere in the neighborhood.
➕ J3 ✉ 900 North Point Street ☎ 415/775 5500
🚋 19, 42

JAPAN CENTER

From kimonos to rice cookers, Japanese arts and crafts are well represented in this complex of stores, restaurants, and offices.
➕ H5 ✉ Post Street, between Buchanan and Webster Streets ☎ 415/922 6776
🚋 2, 3, 4, 38

MACY'S

Occupying two sites on either side of O'Farrell Street, Macy's carries a large stock of quality clothing and much more, not least an inviting array of edibles in the basement food emporium.
➕ K5 ✉ 120 Stockton Street
☎ 415/397 3333 🚋 2, 3, 4, 30, 38, 45

NEIMAN MARCUS

Fine china, dazzling jewelry, and racks of formal evening wear confirm Neiman Marcus as the preferred shopping stop for the wealthy.
➕ K5 ✉ 150 Stockton Street
☎ 415/362 3900 🚋 2, 3, 4, 30, 38, 45

NORDSTROM

A pianist tickles the ivories as shoppers move across this huge store's five floors, whose stock includes a massive selection of shoes.
➕ K5 ✉ San Francisco Shopping Center, 865 Market Street ☎ 415/243 8500
🚋 5, 6, 7, 8, 9, 21, 31, 66, 71
🚠 Powell Street

SAKS FIFTH AVENUE

Less ostentatious than its rivals, Saks offers a strong selection of clothes at prices that may not be low but are reasonable for the quality.
➕ K5 ✉ 384 Post Street
☎ 415/986 4300 🚋 2, 3, 4, 30; Powell–Hyde or Powell–Mason cable car

SAN FRANCISCO SHOPPING CENTER

An architecturally inno-vative home for more than 100 diverse stores.
➕ K5 ✉ 865 Market Street
☎ 415/495 5656
🚋 5, 6, 7, 8, 9, 21, 31, 66, 71
🚠 Powell Street

DISCOUNT OUTLETS & BARGAIN STORES

Numerous factory-outlet stores can be found in SoMa. Many leading design companies discount their damaged or discontinued lines here, and retail operations pass on some of the savings from the area's low rents. Prices are usually 20–50 percent less than in regular stores.

BASIC BROWN BEARS

Open on weekends only, this factory, which makes teddy bears and other small and soft items for children, offers its products at discounted rates and takes customers on a tour of the manufacturing process.

 L8 ✉ 444 De Haro Street ☎ 415/626 0781 🚌 19, 22

ESPRIT DIRECT

This huge warehouse is stocked with cartons of youthful and trendy sports and outdoor wear from the Californian design company. None of it is inexpensive, but much of it is for sale at less than half the normal retail price.

✚ 7M ✉ 499 Illinois Street ☎ 415/957 2550 🚌 15

GOLDEN RAINBOW

This is the city's largest and best discount outlet for children's clothing, up to age 7.

✚ L6 ✉ 435A Brannan Street ☎ 415/543 5191 🚌 15

GUNNE SAX

Standing elbow to elbow with bargain-seeking soon-to-be bridesmaids, you'll find clothes mostly intended for young women and emphasizing traditional styles and a feminine look.

✚ M6 ✉ 35 Stanford Street ☎ 415/495 3326 🚌 15, 32, 42

SIX SIXTY CENTER

A varied selection from men's jackets to women's handbags, children's wear, and all manner of clothing and accessories await discovery here in the bargain outlets spread across the two floors of the Six Sixty Center.

✚ M6 ✉ 660 Third Street ☎ 415/227 0464 🚌 15, 30, 45

THRIFT TOWN

Packed from floor to ceiling with donated secondhand clothing, furniture, books, and lots more, this is one of the largest of San Francisco's thrift stores. You will find many others listed in the phone book.

✚ J8 ✉ 2101 Mission Street ☎ 415/861 1132 🚌 14, 49 Ⓜ 16th Street Mission

YERBA BUENA SQUARE

This contains a varied collection of more than 20 outlet stores, including the Burlington Coat Outlet, which, aside from clothing, boasts a sizable selection of cut-price shoes.

✚ L6 ✉ 899 Howard Street ☎ 415/974 5136 🚌 12

SoMa revived

SoMa highlights the ever-changing nature of San Francisco. In the late 1800s, while the city's rich were building palatial homes on Nob Hill, the flatlands south of Market Street (the area known as SoMa, ▶51) were exclusively the domain of the laboring classes; loading rail and sea cargo continued as SoMa's staple occupation until the 1970s. As the old industries declined, many of the city's discount outlet stores moved into the neighborhood's abandoned warehouses.

ANTIQUES, ART, & COLLECTIBLES

Antique Jackson Square

A historic area with rich pickings for antique searchers, Jackson Square is a compact grouping of mostly brick-built 19th-century structures. The upper levels hold offices, while many ground floors are occupied by the 21 stores that make up the Jackson Square Art & Antiques Dealers Association (414 Jackson Street; ☎ 415/296 8150). Bargains may be few, but 18th- and 19th-century European dressing tables, armchairs and chests of drawers, Turkish rugs, and fine Asian tapestries and decorative pieces are in plentiful supply.

ARTIQUES

Diverse European and American artists are represented in a stock of oil paintings, water-colors, and drawings from the 19th to the mid-20th centuries.
🚋 H4 ✉ 2167 Union Street
☎ 415/929 6969 🚌 41, 45

BEST COMICS AND ROCK ART GALLERY

Anyone drawn to San Francisco for its 1960s hippie associations will relish the reproduction psychedelic posters sold here alongside classic comics.
🚋 J3 ✉ The Cannery, 2801 Leavenworth Street
☎ 415/771 9247 🚌 32; Powell–Hyde cable car

CIRCLE GALLERY

It is hard to predict what might be hanging on the walls of this highly rated gallery, but take the chance to explore inside this landmark Frank Lloyd Wright-designed building (►54).
🚋 K5 ✉ 140 Maiden Lane
☎ 415/989 2100
🚌 2, 3, 4, 30, 45

THE ENCHANTED CRYSTAL

Crystal and glass artfully crafted into decorative objects and jewelry.
🚋 H4 ✉ 1895 Union Street
☎ 415/885 1335
🚌 41, 45

FUMIKI FINE ASIAN ARTS

Japanese *netsuke* and *obi* (the sash for a kimono), Chinese porcelain, and Korean furniture are among the exquisite Far Eastern artifacts to be found in this copiously filled shop.
🚋 H4 ✉ 2001 Union Street
☎ 415/922 0573 🚌 41, 45

GUMP'S

Gump's has been held in high esteem by discerning San Franciscans since 1861; antiques come from all corners of the globe, particularly Asia, an art gallery specializes in the works of emergent artists, and another room is devoted to jade.
🚋 L5 ✉ 240 Post Street
☎ 415/982 1616
🚌 2, 3, 4, 76

LANG ANTIQUES

Diverse but uniformly high-quality merchandise, spanning everything from silver-ware and watches to Russian artworks.
🚋 K5 ✉ 323 Sutter Street
☎ 415/982 2213
🚌 2, 3, 4, 76

PARIS 1925

Admirers of art deco will adore this eye-catching stock of (mostly) art deco-inspired contemporary works and reproductions; there are usually a few authentic period pieces available, too, plus antique timepieces.
🚋 H4 ✉ 1954 Union Street
☎ 415/567 1925
🚌 41, 45

Z GALLERIE

Contemporary design and elaborately framed modern posters and prints for the money-no-object householder.
🚋 H4 ✉ 2071 Union Street
☎ 415/346 9000 🚌 41, 45

BOOKSTORES

A CLEAN WELL-LIGHTED PLACE FOR BOOKS

The city's leading outlet for the newest fiction, be it mainstream or avant-garde, and a selection of nonfiction (►83).
⊞ J6 ✉ 601 Van Ness Avenue ☎ 415/441 6670
🚌 42, 47, 49

A DIFFERENT LIGHT

Generously stocked with fiction and nonfiction titles primarily of interest to gay men, with a section of lesbian-related writing.
⊞ H8 ✉ 489 Castro Street ☎ 415/431 0891 🚌 24

THE BOOKSMITH

Contains a large range of recent general titles on all subjects and several shelves devoted to Californian travel and San Franciscan history.
⊞ G7 ✉ 1644 Haight Street ☎ 415/863 8688 🚌 6, 7, 33, 43, 66, 71

CITY LIGHTS

A bookstore inextricably linked to the 1950s Beat Generation stocking many of the movement's definitive writings, fiction and nonfiction, and literary magazines.
⊞ K4 ✉ 261 Columbus Avenue ☎ 415/362 8193
🚌 15, 41, 83

NATIONAL PARK STORE

Books, magazines, and videos devoted to wild California and the natural history of the American West.
⊞ K 2/3 ✉ Pier 39, Fisherman's Wharf
☎ 415/433 7221 🚌 32

OLD WIVES TALES

Old and new tomes relating to women and women's issues line the shelves of this long-established feminist resource center.
⊞ J 8/9 ✉ 1009 Valencia Street ☎ 415/821 4675
🚌 26

SIERRA CLUB BOOKSTORE

The retail outlet of the publishing wing of the San Francisco-based Sierra Club, one of the country's leading conservation organizations, the bookstore carries numerous titles on the country's wildest and most spectacular regions.
⊞ J6 ✉ 730 Polk Street ☎ 415/923 5600 🚌 19

TILLMAN PLACE BOOKSTORE

Small and homey with knowledgeable staff, this bookstore stocks a tremendous assortment of titles, many of them recent hardbacks, with a special emphasis on travel, history, and biography.
⊞ K5 ✉ 8 Tillman Place ☎ 415/392 4668 🚌 15

WILLIAM K. STOUT ARCHITECTURAL BOOKS

Architectural tomes in sufficient quantity to keep both the professional architect and the interested amateur browsing for hours.
⊞ L4 ✉ 804 Montgomery Street ☎ 415/391 6757
🚌 15, 41

Secondhand books

Besides plentiful outlets for new titles, San Francisco has numerous used bookstores in which dedicated bibliophiles can spend many hours of happy browsing. Recommended stops include Forever After (1475 Haight Street) with diverse fiction and nonfiction; McDonald's Bookshop (48 Turk Street), with books of all kinds and magazines dating back to the 1930s; and Book Bay (Building C, Fort Mason Center), where former library stock is sold at discounted prices.

CLOTHES

Clothes of unusual size

Anyone whose dimensions differ from the average can search for new clothes in San Francisco with confidence. Apparel for large and small men respectively is the business of Rochester Big And Tall (700 Mission Street) and The Short Shop (49 Kearny Street). The Forgotten Woman (550 Sutter Street) and Harper Greer For the Larger Woman (580 Fourth Street) both stock elegant items in large ladies' sizes, while Tall Etc. (61 O'Farrell Street) is for women who reach higher than most.

BANANA REPUBLIC
Noted for its predominantly lightweight, natural-fiber clothing in a range of earth tones for men and women, this outlet offers stylish, comfortable attire for contemporary urban living.

➕ K5 ✉ 256 Grant Street
☎ 415/788 3087 🚌 2, 3, 4

CHANEL BOUTIQUE
Three floors filled with clothes, cosmetics, and much more from the renowned French designer are available for the woman with refined taste.

➕ L5 ✉ 155 Maiden Lane
☎ 415/981 1550
🚌 2, 3, 4, 30, 45

THE HOUND
Offers high-priced, high-quality menswear, much of it based on popular perceptions of what an English country gentleman likes to wear; perfectionists can have their shirts made to measure.

➕ L5 ✉ 111 Sutter Street
☎ 415/989 0429
🚌 2, 3, 4, 76

POSITIVELY HAIGHT STREET
The revival of the tie dyed T-shirt has been a recent San Franciscan phenomenon. This store sells the loudest and boldest examples in the city.

➕ G7 ✉ 1157 Masonic Avenue ☎ 415/252 8747
🚌 6, 7, 33, 43, 66, 71

ROLO
Many Rolo designs take their inspiration from street fashion, conjuring up expensive and extrovert attire for the daring man or woman who wishes to cut a dash on the social circuit.

➕ K7 ✉ 1301 Howard Street
☎ 415/861 1999 🚌 12

VERSUS GIANNI VERSACE
Fans of the top Italian designer can spend a few hundred rather than a few thousand dollars on the elegant (mostly women's) casual wear items. A regular and much more expensive Versace store is around the corner at 70 Post Street.

➕ L5 ✉ Crocker Galleria, 50 Post Street ☎ 415/616 0600
🚌 2, 3, 4, 5, 6

VOGUE ALLEY
Vogue Alley is always worth a browse for its broad range of designer-name women's wear sold at manufacturer's prices.

➕ K5 ✉ 432 Sutter Street
☎ 415/362 7200
🚌 2, 3, 4, 30, 45

WILKES BASHFORD
Classy clothing for men is spread across the six impressively well stocked floors of Wilkes Bashford. The suit section offers complimentary wine or imported mineral water to refresh customers who may be dithering over those crucial decisions of what to buy.

➕ K5 ✉ 375 Sutter Street
☎ 415/986 4380
🚌 2, 3, 4, 30, 45, 76

ACCESSORIES & USED CLOTHES

AARDVARK'S ODD ARK
If looking for a choice of attire of styles from many eras, you will be rewarded by a visit here to the pick of Haight-Ashbury's innumerable used clothing outlets.

G7   1501 Haight Street
415/621 3141   6, 7, 33, 43, 66, 71

BUFFALO EXCHANGE
If you suddenly tire of the clothes you are wearing, this is the place to trade them in and walk out attired in something different; there is always clothing that is just in, or just out, to be picked up for a song—or for a trade-in deal.

G7   1555 Haight Street
415/431 7733   6, 7, 33, 43, 66, 71

DHARMA
Inventive, one-of-a-kind jewelry and other items fuse the counter-culture influences of Haight-Ashbury with the arts and crafts of the Third World at this establishment.

G7   1600 Haight Street
415/621 5597   6, 7, 33, 43, 66, 71

HERMÈS OF PARIS
Nothing comes cheap at this exceedingly posh outlet that features fashions from the famous French designer, but the belts, scarves, gloves, and handbags are small images of perfection.

K5   212 Stockton Street
415/391 7200
2, 3, 4, 30, 45

LA ROSA
Should a formal dinner invitation unexpectedly fall into your hands, this is the perfect spot to hire or buy evening wear that has already seen its share of social occasions; the oldest items generally date from the 1920s.

G7   1711 Haight Street
415/668 3744   6, 7, 33, 43, 66, 71

SPELLBOUND
A general assortment of previously owned clothing, but also an especially fruitful place to hunt down wondrous gowns, hats, and smoking jackets from the 1890s to the 1920s.

F7   1670 Haight Street
415/863 4930   6, 7, 33, 43, 66, 71

TIFFANY & CO
A branch of the revered New York jewelry outlet with more glittering stones than most people can dream about, and a dazzling display of gold and silver ornaments.

K5   350 Post Street
415/781 7000
2, 3, 4, 76

WORN OUT WEST
What started out fulfilling the sartorial needs of gay men in pursuit of the cowboy look has evolved into a cornucopia of high-quality western wear, from Stetson hats and snakeskin boots to exceptionally attractive bolo ties.

H8   582 Castro Street
415/431 6020   24

Markets
Though San Francisco is not known for its markets, fresh fruit, vegetables, and a small amount of seafood can be found at the Farmers' Market held at United Nations Plaza (between Civic Center and Market Street) every Wednesday and Sunday from 7 A.M. Avid market-goers might also like to test their mettle amid the densely packed throng on the Chinatown section of Stockton Street every weekday and Saturday when, it seems, the city's entire Chinese-American population arrives to stock up.

OFFBEAT

Chinatown shops

Exotic, entertaining, and often great value, the shops of Chinatown are among the most interesting in the city. Locals crowd the market stalls along Stockton Street, but nearby Grant Avenue holds visitor-aimed emporia stuffed with anything and everything Asian, from $500 jade ornaments to richly decorated 25¢ chopsticks. More practical but equally intriguing retailers include herbalists Che Sung Tong (729 Washington Street) and the Wok Shop (718 Grant Avenue), with a good line in fearsome meat cleavers.

CANDELIER

Candles will never again seem like ordinary household objects after you view the artful and imaginative varieties sold here.

✚ L5 ✉ 60 Maiden Lane
☎ 415/989 8600
🚌 2, 3, 4, 30, 45

CLARION MUSIC CENTER

Regulars might rent a violin or cello, but casual visitors can content themselves with a stroll along the racks of weird and wonderful Asian musical instruments, which range from Burmese temple bells to Chinese egg rattles.

✚ K4 ✉ 816 Sacramento Street ☎ 415/391 1317
🚌 15, 30, 45

LEFT HAND WORLD

When San Franciscan southpaws feel oppressed by life in a largely right-handed world, they seek solace amid the corkscrews, can openers, and watches all sold here and designed for them.

✚ K2/3 ✉ Pier 39, Fisherman's Wharf
☎ 415/433 3547 🚌 32

THE MUSIC BOX

Be it a ceramic giraffe or a silver cigarette case, every item sold here plays a tune.

✚ H4 ✉ 2201 Union Street ☎ 415/563 5181
🚌 22, 41, 45

PERESTROIKA STORE

Sells a colossal collection of odd items from the former Soviet Union, from hammer-and-sickle T-shirts to elaborate tapestries.

✚ K2/3 ✉ Pier 39, Fisherman's Wharf
☎ 415/788 7043 🚌 32

PIPE DREAMS

A survivor of Haight-Ashbury's 1960s hippie days, the shop continues to cater for the needs of the adventurous smoker and anyone in search of psychedelic ephemera.

✚ G7 ✉ 1376 Haight Street
☎ 415/431 3553 🚌 6, 7, 33, 43, 66, 71

QUANTITY POSTCARDS

A small room lined floor-to-ceiling with postcards of every conceivable kind; the vintage images of San Francisco make amusing, inexpensive souvenirs.

✚ K4 ✉ 1441 Grant Avenue
☎ 415/986 8866 🚌 15, 30, 39, 41, 45

REVIVAL OF THE FITTEST

Glorious cache of mostly 1940s and 1950s Americana: furniture, ornaments, telephones, and all manner of quaint and curious nicknacks.

✚ F7 ✉ 1701 Haight Street
☎ 415/751 8857 🚌 6, 7, 33, 43, 66, 71

YANKEE DOODLE DANDY

Well-stocked with American folk art; sort through the run-of-the-mill objects for the hidden gems; or just admire the traditionally made quilts.

✚ H4 ✉ 1974 Union Street
☎ 415/346 0346 🚌 41, 45

MISCELLANEOUS

ADOLPH GASSER
Spread across 16,000 square feet of retail space, you will find here the largest stock of photographic equipment in northern California.

L5   181 Second Street
  415/495 3852   12, 15

ALFRED DUNHILL OF LONDON
This shop goes entirely against the grain of health-conscious San Francisco, where smoking is decidedly antisocial. Tobacco devotees come here as much to admire the pipes, ashtrays, and quality cigars as to buy the products.

K5   290 Post Street
  415/781 3368
  2, 3, 4, 76

ANSEL ADAMS CENTER SHOP
This photography museum and exhibition space (►42) holds an extensive collection of lavishly illustrated photography-related books and other items with photographic themes.

L6   250 Fourth Street
  415/495 7000   30, 45

COMPUTOWN
San Franciscans looking for the latest software, or just computer equipment generally, swear by the quality, quantity, and low prices here. Good for a browse to see what the wizards of Silicon Valley are up to.

K5   756 Market Street
  415/956 8696   6, 7, 8, 9, 21, 31, 38, 66, 71

FAO SCHWARZ FIFTH AVENUE
When children sleep, they dream of places like this: stuffed to the rafters with huge and imaginative toys from around the world.

K5   48 Stockton Street
  415/394 8700   30, 45

MUSEUM BOOKS
An exemplary collection of art-related books, posters, and souvenirs.

L5   San Francisco Museum of Modern Art, 151 Third Street   415/252 4035
  12, 15, 30, 45, 76

RECKLESS RECORDS
Buys and sells records and CDs, and grades the used items according to their quality, promising a full refund if customers get less than they feel they paid for.

G7   1401 Haight Street
  415/431 3434   6, 7, 33, 43, 66, 71

SAN FRANCISCO OPERA SHOP
Classical music and opera CDs, records and videos, and other performing arts-related souvenir items such as posters and T-shirts.

J6   199 Grove Avenue
  415/565 6414   5, 10, 20, 21, 42, 47, 49, 60, 70, 80
  Civic Center or Van Ness

TEN REN TEA COMPANY
To the delight of visiting tea *aficionados*, this Chinatown store is packed with blends from around the world.

K4   949 Grant Avenue
  415/362 0656
  15, 30, 41

Coffee to go
The city's preponderance of cafés has helped make San Franciscans knowledgeable and discerning coffee drinkers. The expertise extends to the purchase of coffee for brewing at home and the city has acquired several highly regarded outlets for what has been termed "gourmet coffee". One of the most popular is Peet's Coffee And Tea (2156 Chestnut Street and 3419 California Street), stocking beans from around the coffee-growing world together with a formidable variety of grinders and espresso machines.

CLASSICAL MUSIC & PERFORMING ARTS

Tickets

The major ticket agency, BASS, has numerous outlets including the TIX booth on Union Square (see below); Supermail, Four Embarcadero Center; Headlines, 838 Market Street; and The Wherehouse, 165 Kearny Street. For a credit card booking or recorded information: ☎ 510/762 2277. TIX offers half-price day of performance tickets (cash only) for Bay Area arts events from a marked booth on the Stockton Street side of Union Square (☎ 415/433 7827).

Magic Theater

A small theater that has forged an excellent reputation; stages many productions ranging from children's plays to political satire.
➕ H3 ✉ Building D, Fort Mason Center ☎ 415/441 8822 🚌 22, 28, 30, 47, 49

CLUB FUGAZI

A zany revue, *Beach Blanket Babylon*, has been running for 20 years at this North Beach venue, and continues to sell out.
➕ K4 ✉ 678 Green Street ☎ 415/421 4222 🚌 15, 30, 41, 45

CURRAN THEATRE

This is one of several mainstream theaters that are grouped along Geary Street and is the top choice for Broadway blockbusters.
➕ K5 ✉ 445 Geary Street ☎ 415/474 3800 🚌 38

GEARY THEATER

The main base of the American Conservatory Theater, the plays on offer here are highly regarded among knowledgeable theater-goers and critics alike for their highly professional and often thought-provoking productions.
➕ K5 ✉ 415 Geary Street ☎ 415/749 2228 🚌 38

HERBST THEATRE

The theater hosts chamber music, recitals, dance, and jazz throughout the year, and the springtime New and Unusual series from the San Francisco Symphony. The same building's smaller Green Room sees modern experimental pieces performed by San Francisco Contemporary Players.
➕ J6 ✉ War Veterans' Building, 401 Van Ness Avenue ☎ 415/392 4400 🚌 5, 10, 20, 21, 42, 47, 49, 60, 70, 80 🚇 Civic Center or Van Ness

LOUISE M. DAVIES SYMPHONY HALL

This is the home of the San Francisco Symphony orchestra, whose season runs from September to May. Their summer appearances include a Beethoven Festival, a pops series, and a special performance with the Joffrey Ballet.
➕ J6 ✉ 201 Van Ness Avenue ☎ 415/431 5400 🚌 5, 10, 20, 21, 42, 47, 49, 60, 70, 80 🚇 Van Ness or Civic Center

THEATER RHINOCEROS

The home of the USA's first gay and lesbian theater company, the diverse offerings often explore social attitudes and behavior.
➕ J8 ✉ 2926 16th Street ☎ 415/861 5079 🚌 14, 22, 26, 33, 49 🚇 16th Street Mission

WAR MEMORIAL OPERA HOUSE

The Opera House is the venue for the San Francisco Opera's September–December season. Most tickets are sold months in advance, although a limited number of standing tickets are available two hours before a performance. The San Francisco Ballet appears at the same venue from February to May, and returns at Christmas for a performance of *Nutcracker*.
➕ J6 ✉ 301 Van Ness Avenue ☎ 415/864 3330 🚌 5, 10, 20, 21, 42, 47, 49, 60, 70, 80 🚇 Van Ness or Civic Center

ROCK, JAZZ, & BLUES SPOTS

CLUB 181
This small but stylish jazz club mostly features mainstream acts but sometimes switches to jazz-funk or the more esoteric and experimental sounds of acid bop.
➕ K6 ✉ 181 Eddy Street ☎ 415/673 818 🚌 19, 31 🚇 Powell Street

I-BEAM
I-Beam is a bastion of the city's indie rock and grunge scene, often showcasing the best new alternative rock bands in San Francisco and its surrounding area to a mostly youthful audience.
➕ F7 ✉ 1748 Haight Street ☎ 415/668 6006 🚌 6, 7, 66, 71

JAZZ AT PEARL'S
This enjoyable jazz spot draws an informed and appreciative crowd and is a likely place to catch the hottest local—and often national—names.
➕ K4 ✉ 256 Columbus Avenue ☎ 415/291 8255 🚌 41, 83

LOU'S PIER 47
The top-notch blues performers who regularly appear here draw appreciative audiences and are one of the few reasons why San Franciscans mingle with the tourist hordes at Fisherman's Wharf. It offers two shows daily.
➕ J3 ✉ 300 Jefferson Street ☎ 415/771 0377 🚌 32; Powell–Hyde cable car

RASSELAS
At this combined jazz and supper club, you can savor Ethiopian food and listen to some of the better local combos.
➕ G5 ✉ 2801 California Street ☎ 415/567 5010 🚌 1, 4

THE SALOON
This spit-and-sawdust saloon with a history that reaches back to the 1800s makes a great backdrop for no-frills performances by rock and blues bands.
➕ K4 ✉ 1232 Grant Avenue ☎ 415/989 7666 🚌 15, 41, 45, 83

SLIM'S
The excellent sound system and convivial atmosphere make this one of the city's best club-sized music spots for quality rock, jazz, or R&B acts every night.
➕ K7 ✉ 333 Eleventh Street ☎ 415/621 3330 🚌 9, 42

UP & DOWN CLUB
The club is a comfortable and dependable location for enjoying some of the city's most promising jazz performers, and the occasional rock act.
➕ K6 ✉ 1151 Folsom Street ☎ 415/626 2388 🚌 12

THE WARFIELD
A barnlike space that lacks atmosphere, but this is one of the city's major places for the biggest names in rock.
➕ K6 ✉ 982 Market Street ☎ 415/775 7722 🚌 5, 6, 7, 9, 21, 66, 71 🚇 Civic Center or Powell Street

Blues by the bay
Over a weekend each September, the San Francisco Blues Festival brings some of the genre's leading exponents to daylong open-air concerts at Great Meadow, near Fort Mason Center, with a Friday afternoon curtain-raising concert taking place at Justin Herman Plaza, next to the Embarcadero Center.
The enjoyable and relaxed event has been taking place for more than 20 years. For ticket details:
☎ 415/826 6837.

Opening times
Most discos, clubs, and bars open seven nights a week, usually from around 9P.M., but are busiest around midnight.

NIGHTCLUBS

Guided nightclubbing

If deciding where to strut your stuff in the San Franciscan night proves impossible, you might relish the assistance of Three Babes and a Bus (☎ 415/552 CLUB), a company that will carry you—and a busload of similarly indecisive individuals—on a four-hour tour of some of the city's hottest nightspots (Fridays and Saturdays only). The $30 price includes admission and special ID allowing you to walk straight in, even when there is a line.

BAHIA TROPICAL
Live and recorded Brazilian beats and red-hot salsa rhythms make this the best place in the city for genuine dance enthusiasts with energy to burn.
➕ J7 ✉ 1600 Market Street ☎ 415/861 8657 🚌 6, 7, 66, 71 🚋 Van Ness

CESAR'S LATIN PALACE
Legendary Hispanic hot-spot for salsa, jazz, and funk: the rhythms are eagerly lapped up by a sharply dressed, hedonistic crowd.
➕ J10 ✉ 3140 Mission Street ☎ 648 6611 🚌 14, 49 🚋 24th Street Mission

CLUB DV8
The latest and grooviest dance sounds attract an arty and alternative crowd, as do the regular poetry readings, tattooings, and other bizarre events that take place in the side rooms.
➕ L5 ✉ 540 Howard Street ☎ 415/777 1419 🚌 12

DNA LOUNGE
A noted indie rock music venue and one where the seemingly nocturnal doyens of the city's cultural cutting edge gather to pose and strut. Depending on the night of the week, all manner of weird and wonderful avant-garde acts appear here.
➕ K7 ✉ 375 Eleventh Street ☎ 415/626 1409 🚌 9, 42

END-UP
Biggest and most dependable of a number of gay- and lesbian-oriented nightspots, with riotous dance music every night.
➕ L6 ✉ 995 Harrison Street ☎ 415/543 7700 🚌 27, 42

JOHNNY LOVE'S
Smoothly sophisticated and unrepentantly upscale, this is the nighttime haunt of San Francisco's rich and beautiful, and those who like to be seen among them.
➕ J4 ✉ 1500 Broadway ☎ 451/931 6053 🚌 83

OZ
A wealthy and sophisticated crowd gathers to dance away the night on this high-class hotel's 32nd floor, where the disco replicates a woodland glade in sumptuous style.
➕ K5 ✉ Westin St Francis Hotel, 335 Powell Street at Union Square ☎ 415/774 0116 🚌 2, 3, 4, 6, 38, 71; Powell–Hyde and Powell–Mason cable cars

PARADISE LOUNGE
Multi-roomed club where the young and determinedly cool patrons can rove between dance floors, live band areas, and pool halls.
➕ K7 ✉ 1501 Folsom Street ☎ 415/861 6906 🚌 12

PAULA'S CLUBHOUSE
Each night brings a different theme to this former fire station with a packed dance floor and top-notch sound system.
➕ J8 ✉ 3160 16th Street ☎ 415/451 1617 🚋 16th Street Mission 🚌 22

BARS

CARNELIAN ROOM

A stylish and upscale (evening only) bar on this landmark building's 52nd floor, with wonderful sunset views across the city.

🏠 L5 ✉ Bank of America HQ, 555 California Street ☎ 415/433 7500 🚌 15, 42; California Street cable car

GORDON BIERSCH BREWERY

Fine lagers and ales brewed on the premises make this a favorite of the Financial District's well dressed after-work crowd; weekends are more varied and relaxed.

🏠 M5 ✉ 2 Harrison Street ☎ 415/243 8246 🚌 32, 42

LI PO'S

A cavelike entrance leads into the interior of this Chinatown bar, where the over-the-top decor seems less extreme after a few Chinese Tsing Tao beers.

🏠 K4 ✉ 916 Grant Avenue ☎ 415/982 0072 🚌 1, 15, 30, 45

MAXFIELD'S BAR & GRILL

Sip a cocktail in subdued surroundings and gaze over the immense Maxfield Parrish mural behind the bar.

🏠 L5 ✉ Sheraton Palace Hotel, 2 New Montgomery Street ☎ 415/392 8600 🚌 5, 6, 7, 8, 9, 21, 31, 38, 42, 45, 71

PERRY'S

Made its name as a singles bar for the affluent of Pacific Heights but is now more a friendly neighborhood watering hole that attracts a solvent mid-30s crowd.

🏠 H4 ✉ 1944 Union Street ☎ 415/922 9022 🚌 41, 45

REDWOOD ROOM

A 1930s art deco room decorated with Gustav Klimt prints; recline in the deep armchairs and imbibe the atmosphere.

🏠 K5 ✉ Four Seasons Clift Hotel, 495 Geary Street ☎ 415/775 4700 🚌 38

S. HOLMES ESQ. PUBLIC HOUSE AND DRINKING SALON

An average hotel bar improved by impressive views and an extraordinary collection of Sherlock Holmes memorabilia.

🏠 K5 ✉ Holiday Inn, 480 Sutter Street ☎ 415/398 8900 🚌 2, 3, 4, 76

SAN FRANCISCO BREWING COMPANY

Serves a selection of excellent own-brew beers and has live music several nights a week; very busy on weekday evening rush hours and Friday and Saturday nights.

🏠 K4 ✉ 155 Columbus Avenue ☎ 415/434 3344 🚌 15, 41

TORONADO

The various alternative lifestyles that are part and parcel of the Haight-Ashbury neighborhood can be observed at this lively haunt.

🏠 H7 ✉ 547 Haight Street ☎ 415/863 2276 🚌 6, 7, 66, 71

Liquor laws

Bars can legally be open at any time between 6 A.M. and 2 A.M., though most choose to open their doors around 11 A.M. and close them around midnight (later on Fridays and Saturdays). Provided they are licensed, restaurants can serve alcohol throughout their hours of business except between 2 A.M. and 6 A.M. To buy or consume alcohol legally, customers must be age 21 or older. In a bar, nightclub or restaurant, youthful-looking patrons may well be asked to show proof of their age.

Cafés for Entertainment

Inside cafés

San Francisco is renowned for its proliferation of loosely European-style cafés, found in every neighborhood, and there is no better place to check the pulse of the city. Along with quality coffee and a selection of wholesome snacks, cafés typically provide newspapers (and sometimes books) for their customers; some are noted for their pickup chess games, others for their ambient music or computer with access to the Internet. Uninteresting cafés quickly go out of business.

CAFÉ FLORE
The variety of affectionate nicknames applied to this energetic spot—such as Café Haircut and Café Bore—reflect its popularity among a predominantly gay clientele.
✚ H8　✉ 2298 Market Street
☎ 415/621 8579　🚃 8, 37;
J, K, L, M, N

CAFÉ PICARO
San Franciscan Bohemia is now to be found in the Mission District, which attracts a diverse assortment of ageing Beats, radical writers, and avant-garde artists.
✚ J8　✉ 3120 16th Street
☎ 415/431 4089　🚃 22

CAFFÈ MALVINA
The slightly austere interior is of this café is made more welcoming by large windows overlooking Washington Square.
✚ K4　✉ 1600 Stockton
Street　☎ 415/391 1290
🚃 15, 30, 39, 41, 45,

CAFFÈ ROMA
This is a relative newcomer and worth visiting for its cupid murals alone.
✚ K4　✉ 414 Columbus
Avenue　☎ 415/391 8584
🚃 15, 30, 41, 45

LE PETIT CAFÉ
Despite doing much of its trade as a restaurant, this two-room café comes close to encapsulating the character of affluent and arty Russian Hill.
✚ J4　✉ 2164 Larkin Street
☎ 415/776 5356
🚃 19, 41, 45

LOVE 'N HAIGHT
This is a favorite haunt of the Lower Haight area's youthful and countercultural population, fueling a dressed-down crowd with quality coffee and Middle Eastern snacks.
✚ H7　✉ 553 Haight
Street　☎ 415/252 8190
🚃 6, 7, 22, 66, 71

THE ORBIT ROOM
Larger and more eclectic than the usual café, meriting a stop for the chrome fittings that evoke a 1940s sci-fi mood.
✚ J7　✉ 1900 Market Street
☎ 415/252 9525　🚃 8; F

SACRED GROUNDS
Occasional weekend live events, but always a good place to mingle among chess players and aspiring intellectuals.
✚ F7　✉ 2095 Hayes Street
☎ 415/387 3895　🚃 21

TOSCA CAFÉ
Opened in 1917 and allegedly serving the first espresso in California, Tosca has opera reverberating from its jukebox and numerous celebrity regulars.
✚ K4　✉ 242 Columbus
Avenue　☎ 415/986 9651
🚃 15, 41

VESUVIO'S
A legendary haunt of the original Beats, Vesuvio's is still the scene of earnest debate and philosophical conversations.
✚ K4　✉ 255 Columbus
Avenue　☎ 415/362 3370
🚃 15, 41, 83

OTHER IDEAS

A CLEAN WELL-LIGHTED PLACE FOR BOOKS

An impressive assortment of authors, local and national, show up at this bookstore for signings, readings, and talks.

✚ J6 ✉ 601 Van Ness Avenue ☎ 415/441 6670 🚌 42, 47, 49

ABOVE PARADISE

A room above the Paradise Lounge nightclub where poets, and would-be poets, can recite their latest verses to anyone who is interested; usually operates one night a week—phone for details.

✚ K7 ✉ 1501 Folsom Street ☎ 415/861 6906 🚌 12

CASTRO THEATRE

A 1920s movie palace, complete with Wurlitzer organ, which makes an atmospheric setting for a daily diet of cult and revival movies.

✚ H8 ✉ 429 Castro Street ☎ 415/612 6120 🚌 24; K, L, M

CLAY

The city's oldest continuously running movie theater, in business since 1910, and a favorite with San Franciscan film buffs as the main showcase for first-run foreign films.

✚ H5 ✉ 2261 Fillmore Street ☎ 415/346 1123 🚌 3, 22

COBB'S

Nationally known names top the bill at this popular 200-seat comedy club every night

except the Monday "open mic" nights. Book in advance for the leading draws.

✚ J3 ✉ The Cannery, 2801 Leavenworth Street ☎ 415/928 4320 🚌 32

HOLY CITY ZOO

Likable, small comedy club that showcases the city's rising stars and that made a name for itself by giving Robin Williams an early break.

✚ E6 ✉ 408 Clement Street ☎ 415/386 4242 🚌 2

JOSIE'S CABARET AND JUICE JOINT

Well-regarded club for song, dance, and comedy, often with a gay and lesbian orientation.

✚ H8 ✉ 3583 16th Street ☎ 415/861 7933 🚌 22, 37; K, L, M

KABUKI 8

This eight-screen modernistic cinema complex in the heart of Japantown is the likeliest spot to find the latest Hollywood movies.

✚ H5 ✉ 1881 Post Street, between Buchanan and Webster Streets ☎ 415/931 9800 🚌 2, 3, 4, 38

SAN FRANCISCO ART INSTITUTE

Riotous Thursday evenings find poets, comics, and anyone with something to say grabbing the microphone and, they hope, the audience's attention.

✚ J3 ✉ 800 Chestnut Street ☎ 415/771 7020 🚌 15, 30, 41; Powell–Hyde cable car

Spectator sports

The San Francisco 49ers and the San Francisco Giants both play their matches at Candlestick Park, eight miles south of the city. Some tickets for the 49ers may be available through agencies but most games sell out far in advance. Giants' tickets are more readily available, either from the stadium box office (☎ 415/467 8000) or through BASS Ticketmaster (☎ 510/762 2277).

Stern Grove concerts

On Sunday afternoons from June to August, a eucalyptus-shrouded natural amphitheater at Stern Grove offers free concerts and performances ranging from classical music and opera to jazz and modern dance.

✚ Off map ✉ Sloat Boulevard at 19th Avenue ☎ 415/398 6551 🚌 28

LUXURY HOTELS

Prices

You may expect to pay the following prices:

Luxury hotels—over $140

Moderate hotels—up to $80

Budget hotels—up to $40

Hostels—$12 per person

Prices are per night minima, based (except for hostels) on two people sharing.

Hotel telephone numbers

Many hotels and some bed and breakfast inns can be telephoned using toll-free numbers. Remember that they can usually be dialed from anywhere in the United States or Canada, although there is sometimes a different toll-free number for calls made within California (and a few may be available in California only). Overall, they provide a good way to do long-term planning.

CAMPTON PLACE
Excellently placed, with stylish rooms and impeccable service.
✚ K5 ✉ 40 Stockton Street ☎ toll-free in California 800/235 4300, in USA 800/426 3135; or 415/781 5555 🍴 Excellent restaurant ($$/$$$) 🚌 30, 45

HOTEL NIKKO
An ultramodern hotel boasting every conceivable facility.
✚ K5 ✉ 222 Mason Street ☎ toll-free 800/645 5687; or 415/394 1111 🍴 Very good café ($$) and excellent restaurant ($$$) 🚌 27, 38

INN AT THE OPERA
Quiet and elegant, and a favorite of thespians and opera stars for its proximity to the performing-arts halls of Civic Center.
✚ J6 ✉ 333 Fulton Street ☎ toll-free in California 800/325 2708, in USA 800/423 9610; or 415/863 8400 🍴 Excellent restaurant ($$$) 🚌 5, 21

MANDARIN ORIENTAL
Sizable and opulently furnished rooms; some bathrooms have fabulous city views.
✚ L5 ✉ 222 Sansome Street ☎ 415/885 0999 🍴 Excellent restaurant ($$/$$$) 🚌 42

THE MIYAKO
Fusing the ideas of East and West, some rooms are designed in traditional Japanese style with tatami mats and futons.
✚ H5 ✉ 1625 Post Street ☎ 800/533 4567; or 415/922 3200 🍴 Excellent restaurant ($$/$$$) 🚌 2, 3, 4

RITZ-CARLTON
Sumptuous rooms; on-site fitness center and swimming pool.
✚ K5 ✉ 600 Stockton Street ☎ 800/241 3333; or 415/296 7465 🍴 Two excellent restaurants (both $$$) 🚌 30, 45; California Street cable car

SHERATON PALACE
A stunning $60-million renovation of the city's first luxury hotel.
✚ L5 ✉ 2 New Montgomery Street ☎ 800/325 3535; or 415/392 8600 🍴 Three excellent restaurants (all $$$) 🚌 5, 6, 7, 8, 9, 21, 31, 38, 42, 45, 71 🚇 Montgomery Street

THE SHERMAN HOUSE
A lovingly restored 1870s mansion in an exclusive residential area.
✚ H4 ✉ 2160 Green Street ☎ 415/563 3600 🍴 Excellent restaurant ($$$); breakfast included 🚌 22, 24, 41, 45

WESTIN ST. FRANCIS
A San Franciscan landmark since 1904 and resoundingly aristocratic.
✚ K5 ✉ 335 Powell Street at Union Square ☎ 800/228 3000; or 415/397 7000 🍴 Very good café ($$) 🚌 2, 3, 4, 6, 38, 71; Powell–Hyde and Powell–Mason cable cars

WHITE SWAN INN
English antiques, furnishings, and paintings contribute to the mood of low-key elegance in this 1908 building.
✚ K5 ✉ 845 Bush Street ☎ 415/775 1755 🍴 Breakfast and afternoon tea included 🚌 2, 3, 4, 27, 76

MID-RANGE HOTELS

ALAMO SQUARE INN
On scenic Alamo Square and offering a choice of antiques-filled or high-tech accommodations in two adjoining Victorians.
✚ H6 ✉ 719 Scott Street ☎ 800/345 9888; or 415/992 2055 🍴 Breakfast and evening wine included 🚌 21

ARCHBISHOP'S MANSION INN
Dating from 1904 and transformed from a genuine archbishop's residence to an inn with 15 antiques-filled rooms.
✚ H6 ✉ 1000 Fulton Street ☎ toll-free in California 800/543 5820; or 415/563 7872 🍴 Breakfast included 🚌 5, 21

PHOENIX INN
An upbeat color scheme, heated outdoor pool, and relaxed mood make this popular with visiting rock stars.
✚ J6 ✉ 601 Eddy Street ☎ 800/CITYINN; or 415/776 1380 🍴 Good restaurant ($$); breakfast included 🚌 19, 31

THE QUEEN ANNE
Formerly a girls' school, this Victorian building on the edge of Japan-town offers comfortable high-ceilinged rooms.
✚ J5 ✉ 1590 Sutter Street ☎ 800/227 3970; or 415/441 2828 🍴 Breakfast and afternoon tea included 🚌 2, 3, 4, 76

THE RED VICTORIAN
The quintessential Californian experience; the guest rooms are situated above a gallery of Meditative Art and a wholefood café.
✚ F/G 7 ✉ 1665 Haight Street ☎ 415/864 1978 🍴 Breakfast included 🚌 6, 7, 43, 66, 71

STANYAN PARK HOTEL
A small hotel with a friendly mood; adjacent to Golden Gate Park.
✚ F7 ✉ 750 Stanyan Street ☎ 415/751 1000 🍴 Breakfast included 🚌 6, 7, 33, 43, 66, 71

TRITON
With bold and arty designs throughout, this is tailor-made for the trend-conscious traveler.
✚ K5 ✉ 342 Grant Avenue ☎ 800/433 6611; 415/394 0500 🍴 Good café ($$) 🚌 2, 3, 4, 76

VICTORIAN INN ON THE PARK
A lovely rambling 19th-century house with 12 antiques-furnished rooms.
✚ G7 ✉ 301 Lyon Street ☎ toll-free in California 800/435 1967; or 415/931 1830 🍴 Breakfast and evening wine included 🚌 21

VINTAGE COURT
Classy and comfortable, with rooms labeled not with numbers but with the names of selected Wine Country wineries.
✚ K5 ✉ 650 Bush Street ☎ 800/654 1100; or 415/392 4666 🍴 Excellent restaurant ($$$); complimentary evening wine 🚌 2, 3, 4, 30, 76

WASHINGTON SQUARE INN
Homey and in an ideal North Beach location.
✚ K4 ✉ 1660 Stockton Street ☎ toll-free in California 800/388 0220; or 415/981 4220 🍴 Breakfast and afternoon tea included 🚌 15, 30, 39, 41, 45

Bookings

Reservations can be made by phone, fax, or mail, and should be made as early as possible. A deposit (usually by credit card) equivalent to the nightly rate will ensure your room is held at least until 6P.M.; if you are arriving later, inform the hotel. Credit card is the usual payment method; traveler's checks or cash can be used but payment will then be expected in advance. The total charge will include the city's 12 percent accommodations tax.

BUDGET ACCOMMODATIONS

Bed and breakfast

San Francisco's bed-and-breakfast inns, typically converted Victorian homes sumptuously furnished and stuffed with antiques, offer a friendly alternative to hotels. B&B owners will often attend to guests personally, serving them a healthy homecooked breakfast, and will readily pass on their knowledge of the city. Reflecting the fact that both the individual properties and the rooms within them can vary greatly, B&Bs spanning all price categories are found all over the city. Advance booking is always recommended. B&B accommodation can be arranged through:

Bed & Breakfast International

✉ PO Box 282910, San Francisco, CA 94128-2910

☎ 800/696 1690, reservations 800/872 4500

Bed & Breakfast San Francisco

☎ PO Box 420009, San Francisco, CA 94142

☎ 415/479 1913

AMSTERDAM HOTEL
Good value, pleasantly furnished rooms located just below the crest of Nob Hill.
➕ K5 ✉ 749 Taylor Street ☎ 800/637 3444; or 415/673 3277 🍴 Breakfast included 🚍 2, 3, 4, 76

BRADY ACRES
With microwave ovens and coffee makers, the rooms resemble small self-contained apartments; in keeping with this, guest services are few but prices low.
➕ K5 ✉ 649 Jones Street ☎ 800/627 2396; or 415/929 8033 🚍 27, 38, 76

GRANT PLAZA
In the heart of Chinatown, offering small but nicely furnished rooms with private bathrooms.
➕ K5 ✉ 465 Grant Avenue ☎ toll-free 800/472 6899; or 415/434 3883 🚍 15, 30, 45

24 HENRY
A friendly five-room guest house in the Castro district, run by and chiefly aimed at gay men.
➕ H7 ✉ 24 Henry Street ☎ toll-free 800/900 5686; or 415/864 5686 🍴 Breakfast included 🚍 24, 37

INTER-CLUB/GLOBE HOSTEL
Pitched at globetrotting backpackers (U.S. citizens must show evidence of recent foreign travel), this welcoming hostel has small dorms, safety deposit boxes, and no curfew.
➕ K6 ✉ 10 Hallam Place ☎ 415/431 0540 🍴 Coffee 🚍 12

MARINA MOTEL
Plain and simple motel on the north edge of Pacific Heights, with a choice of regular and kitchen-equipped rooms.
➕ G4 ✉ 2576 Lombard Street ☎ 800/346 6118; or 415/921 9406 🚍 28, 43, 76

MARY ELIZABETH INN
For women only, this Edwardian building with unobtrusive Methodist church connections provides a quiet base.
➕ K5 ✉ 1040 Bush Street ☎ 415/673 6768 🍴 Two daily meals included 🚍 27

SAN FRANCISCO INTERNATIONAL HOSTEL
The largest youth hostel in the USA, with small dormitories, laundry facilities, and a great view across the Golden Gate. Advance reservations only and a three-night limit in summer.
➕ H3 ✉ Building 240, Fort Mason ☎ 415/771 7277 🍴 Kitchens 🚍 28, 49

SAN REMO HOTEL
A fully renovated 1906 Italianate villa between North Beach and Fisherman's Wharf with simple but appealing rooms (few with bathrooms) grouped around a central atrium.
➕ K3 ✉ 2237 Mason Street ☎ 800/352 7365; or 415/776 8688 🚍 15, 30, 39, 41

SAN FRANCISCO's
travel facts

ARRIVING & DEPARTING

When to go

- Tourist months are July and August.
- September and October are better times to visit—the weather is like Indian summer, and the crowds have thinned.
- San Francisco's many festivals and events occur throughout the year.

Climate

- San Francisco's climate is generally mild. Morning and evening fogs hold the temperature down between June and August, causing September and October to be the city's sunniest—and most enjoyable—months.
- Bring a sweater or jacket for evening outings.
- An umbrella is always useful; most rainfall occurs between November and March.

Arriving by air

- The major gateway to San Francisco is the San Francisco International Airport (☎ 415/761 0800), just south of the city, off U.S. 101. Several domestic airlines serve the Oakland Airport (☎ 415/577 4000), which is across the bay but not much farther away from downtown San Francisco (via I–880 and I–80), although traffic on the Bay Bridge may at times make travel time longer. Flying time is five hours from New York, four hours from Chicago, and one hour from Los Angeles.
- Carriers serving San Francisco include Alaska Air (☎ 800/426 0333), American (☎ 800/433 7300), Continental (☎ 800/525 0280),

Delta (☎ 800/221 1212), Southwest (☎ 800/435 9792), TWA (☎ 800/221 2000), United (☎ 800/241 6522), and USAir (☎ 800/428 4322).

- For inexpensive, no-frills flights, contact **Midwest Express** (☎ 800/452 2022), based in Milwaukee, which serves 45 U.S. cities in the Midwest and on both coasts, including San Francisco; and **Private Jet** (☎ 404/231 7571, 800/546 7571, or 800/949 9400), based in Atlanta, serving San Francisco.
- Privately-run minibuses will pick up passengers from the traffic island directly outside the terminal.
- The SFO Airporter coach (☎ 415/495 8404) runs every 20 minutes between 5AM and 11PM from the airport to hotels around Union Square; fare is currently $8 (round-trip $14).
- Depending on traffic conditions, a taxi into the city will cost $30–$40.
- Airport information 415/761 0800; Super Shuttle ☎ 415/558 8500.
- To register complaints about charter and scheduled airlines, contact the U.S. Department of Transportation's **Office of Consumer Affairs** (400 7th St. NW, Washington, DC 20590, ☎ 202/366 2220 or 800/322 7873).
- An established consolidator selling to the public is TFI Tours International (34 W. 32nd St., New York, NY 10001, ☎ 212/736 1140 or 800/745 8000).

Arriving by bus

- Greyhound buses into San Francisco terminate at the Transbay Terminal, First and Mission Streets.
- Information ☎ 415/558 6789.

Arriving by train

- Passengers disembark east of the city at Emeryville and continue to San Francisco's Transbay Terminal by free shuttle bus.
- Information ☎ 800/872 7245.

ESSENTIAL FACTS

Travel insurance

- Travel insurance covering baggage, health, and trip cancellation or interruptions is available from: **Access America** (Box 90315, Richmond, VA 23286, ☎ 804/285 3300 or 800/284 8300), **Carefree Travel Insurance** (Box 9366, 100 Garden City Plaza, Garden City, NY 11530, ☎ 516/294 0220 or 800/323 3149), **Near Travel Service** (Box 1339, Calumet City, IL 60409, ☎ 708/868 6700 or 800/654 6700), **Tele-Trip** (Mutual of Omaha Plaza, Box 31716, Omaha, NE 68131, ☎ 800/228 9792), **Travel Insured International** (Box 280568, East Hartford, CT 06128 0568, ☎ 203/528 7663 or 800/243 3174), **Travel Guard International** (1145 Clark St., Stevens Point, WI 54481 ☎ 715/345 0505 or 800/826 1300), and **Wallach & Company** (107 W. Federal St., Box 480, Middleburg, VA 22117, ☎ 703/687 3166 or 800/237 6615).

Average opening hours

- Stores: Mon–Sat 9 or 10 to 5 or 6. Department stores, shopping centers, and shops aimed at tourists in Fisherman's Wharf and Chinatown keep longer hours and are also open on Sundays.
- Banks: Mon–Fri 9–3 or 3:30; some branches open until 5PM once a week.

Public holidays

- New Year's Day (Jan 1)
- Martin Luther King Day (third Monday in Jan)
- President's Day (third Monday in Feb)
- Memorial Day (third Monday in May)
- Independence Day (Jul 4)
- Labor Day (first Monday in Sep)
- Columbus Day (second Monday in Oct)
- Veterans' Day (Nov 1)
- Thanksgiving Day (fourth Thursday in Nov)
- Christmas Day (Dec 25)

Money matters

- Nearly all banks have Automatic Teller Machines (ATMs) which accept cards linked to the Cirrus or Plus networks. Before leaving home, check which network your cards are linked to, and ensure your personal identification number is valid.
- For specific Cirrus locations in the United States and Canada, call 800/424 7787. For U.S. Plus locations, call 800/843 7587 and enter the area code and first three digits of the number you're calling from (or of the calling area where you want an ATM).
- Credit cards are widely accepted and a secure alternative to cash.
- An 8.5% sales tax is added to marked retail prices.
- Funds can be wired via **American Express MoneyGram** (☎ 800/926 9400 from the U.S. and Canada for locations and information) or **Western Union** (☎ 800/325 6000 for agent locations or to send using MasterCard or Visa, 800/321 2923 in Canada).

Single travelers

- Single travelers, especially women traveling alone, are not unusual in

San Francisco. Unwelcome attention is not unknown, however, and in areas such as the Tenderloin and parts of the Mission District and Western Addition, lone females should be especially cautious.

Etiquette

- Be aware of the antismoking feeling that prevails in San Francisco. Be sure to check whether smoking is frowned upon—or even illegal—before you light up inside a building.
- Tip at least 15 percent in a restaurant; 15–20 percent of a taxi fare; $1 per bag to a porter.

Student travelers

- To get discounts on transportation and admissions, get the **International Student Identity** Card (ISIC) if you're a bona fide student or the **International Youth Card** (IYC) if you're under 26. In the United States, the ISIC and IYC cards cost $16 each and include basic travel accident and illness coverage, plus a toll-free travel hot line. Apply through the **Council on International Educational Exchange** (CIEE, 205 E. 42nd St., 16th Floor, New York, NY 10017, ☎ 212/661 1450) with locations in Boston (729 Boylston St., Boston, MA 02116, ☎ 617/266 1926), Miami (9100 S. Dadeland Blvd., Miami, FL 33156, ☎ 305/670 9261), Los Angeles (1093 Broxton Ave., Los Angeles, CA 90024, ☎ 310/208 3551), 43 college towns nationwide, and the United Kingdom (28A Poland St., London W1V 3DB, ☎ 0171/437 7767). Twice a year, it publishes *Student Travels* magazine. The CIEE's Council Travel Service offers

domestic air passes for bargain travel within the United States and is the exclusive U.S. agent for several student-discount cards.
- Anyone aged under 21 is forbidden to buy alcohol and may be denied admission to some nightclubs.

Time differences

- San Francisco is three hours behind the East Coast.

Rest Rooms

- Public buildings are obliged to provide rest rooms, which are almost always maintained in immaculate condition as are those in hotel lobbies, restaurants, and most bars.

PUBLIC TRANSPORTATION

- Much of San Francisco can be explored comfortably by walking, but the city has an excellent public transportation system made up of buses, cable cars, and the underground BART system.
- MUNI (buses and cable cars) ☎ 415/673 MUNI.
- A partially underground street car system serves the outer neighborhoods, but is unlikely to be of great use to visitors. Taxis need only be used if you are in a rush, traveling late at night when public transportation services are skeletal, or to pass quickly through unsalubrious neighborhoods.

Cable cars

- Cable cars are more of a tourist attraction than a practical means of getting around and

operate on just three routes:
two (Powell–Mason and
Powell–Hyde) run between
Market Street and Fisherman's
Wharf, and another (California
Street) runs between the
Financial District and Nob Hill.
- Tickets cost $2 per ride and
should be bought from the
self-service machines at the
end of each route, or from the
conductor when you board.
Cable cars operate between
6A.M. and 1A.M.

Buses
- Buses cover the entire city.
- The flat fare is currently $1; to
change buses on a single ride,
ask the driver for a free transfer
ticket. Exact change (coins or a
dollar bill) is necessary and should
be fed into the machine next to
the driver when boarding.
- Buses operate 5AM–1AM; outside
these hours a reduced frequency
service on the main routes is
provided by the so-called
"Owl Service" buses.

BART
- The swift and efficient Bay
Area Rapid Transit (BART)
system is chiefly of use for
crossing the bay to Berkeley
and Oakland, though it also
runs through the city and forms
a speedy link between the
Financial District, Civic Center
and the Mission District.
- Fares range from 80¢ to $3
according to distance traveled.
Tickets can be bought from
machines at BART stations.
- The BART system runs
Mon–Fri 4A.M.–midnight;
Sat 6A.M.–midnight;
Sun 8A.M.–midnight.
- BART Information
☎ 415/788 BART.

Schedule & map information
- Bus routes are shown in the
phone book and at most bus
stops. Detailed maps and time-
tables are available from City
Hall and, in a style more
accessible for visitors (and
including BART routes), from
the Visitor Information Center
on Hallidie Plaza.
- All BART stations display
detailed maps of the BART
system.

Ticket discounts
- A MUNI Passport, valid on all
MUNI services (buses and
cable cars) for one, three, or
seven days, currently costs $6,
$10, or $15 respectively. The
MUNI Passport can be bought at
the Visitor Information Center
(✉ Hallidie Plaza), TIX Outlet
(✉ Union Square facing
Stockton Street), or from MUNI
(✉ Room 238, 949 Presidio
Avenue).
- Not valid on cable cars is a one-
day MUNI pass costing $2.25.

Taxis
- Taxis can be hailed in the street
or from taxi stands at major
hotels and at transport terminals.
- During rush hours (7–9 and 4–6)
and rain showers it is notoriously
hard to find a free taxi cruising
the streets. Average taxi fares
are $1.90 for the first mile
and $1.50 for each additional
mile.
- Hotel receptionists will
routinely order a taxi for you
on request. Alternatively you
can phone one of the following
firms:
De Soto (☎ 415/673 1414);
Luxor (☎ 415/282 4141);
Veteran's (☎ 415/552 1300);
Yellow (☎ 415/626 2345).

91

MEDIA & COMMUNICATIONS

Telephones

- Public telephones are found in the street, in hotel lobbies, restaurants, and most public buildings.
- Local calls cost 25¢.
- Calls from hotel room phones are liable to be much more expensive than those made on a public phone.
- The area code for San Francisco is 415. The code for Berkeley and Oakland is 510.

Post offices

- Most post offices are open Monday to Friday from 8A.M. to 6P.M. and on Saturdays from 8A.M. to 1P.M. For information: ☎ 415/556 2500.

Newspapers

- San Francisco has two daily newspapers, the morning *San Francisco Chronicle* and the afternoon *San Francisco Examiner* (combined on Sundays), and two major free weekly newspapers, *SF Weekly* and *San Francisco Bay Guardian*.

Magazines

- Free tourist-aimed magazines are found in hotel lobbies; their discount coupons can save money on sightseeing and food.

Television

- Linked to national networks, the main San Francisco TV channels are:
  2 KTVU (FOX),
  4 KRON (NBC),
  5 KPIX (CBS),
  7 KGO (ABC), and
  9 KQED (PBS).

EMERGENCIES

Sensible precautions

- San Francisco is one of the country's safest cities but the Tenderloin, and parts of the Western Addition and Mission District, may seem (and may be) threatening, especially after dark. Discuss your itinerary with your hotel's reception staff to point out any potential problems.
- Do not carry easily snatched bags and cameras, or stuff your wallet into your back pocket. In a bar or restaurant, keep your belongings within sight and within reach.
- Keep valuables in the hotel's safe and never carry more money than you need. Wads of cash are seldom necessary, and it is safer to make major purchases with traveler's checks or credit cards.
- Lost traveler's checks are relatively quick and easy to replace. Keep the numbers of the checks separate from the checks.
- If only in order to make an insurance claim, you should report any item stolen to the nearest police precinct (the address of which will be in the phone book). It is highly unlikely that any stolen goods will be recovered, but the police will be able to fill out the forms that your insurance company will need.

Lost property

- San Francisco International Airport: ☎ 415/876 2424.
- MUNI buses or cable cars: ☎ 415/923 6168.
- Otherwise call the relevant police station; the local precinct's number will be in the phone book.

Medical treatment

- Find a doctor by looking under "Physicians and Surgeons" or "Dentists" in *Yellow Pages*. Alternatively, phone the San Francisco Medical Society (☎ 415/567 6230) for doctor referral or the San Francisco Dental Society (☎ 415/421 1435) to find a dentist.
- Most city hospitals accept emergency cases. Those with well-equipped 24-hour casualty departments are: San Francisco General ✉ 1001 Potrero Avenue (☎ 415/206 8000); and St. Francis Memorial Hospital ✉ 900 Hyde Street (☎ 415/775 4321).

Medicines

- Pharmacies are plentiful in San Francisco (and listed in *Yellow Pages* under "Drugstores").
- If you are using medication regularly, the safest course is to bring a supply with you.
- There are several late-night pharmacies in the city. One of them, Walgreen, offers a round-the- clock service at two locations: ✉ 3201 Divisadero Street (☎ 415/931 6417), and ✉ 498 Castro Street (☎ 415/861 3136).

Emergency telephone numbers

- Fire, police, or ambulance: ☎ 911 (no money required).
- Rape Crisis Hotline: ☎ 415/647 7273.
- 24-hour Crisis Line: ☎ 415/777 9696,
- Travelers Aid: ☎ 415/781 6738.

VISITOR INFORMATION

- Contact the **San Francisco Convention and Visitor Bureau** (201 3rd St., Suite 900, 94103, ☎ 415/974 6900). The attractive 80-page *San Francisco Book* ($2; from the SFCVB at Box 6977, 94101) includes up-to-date information on theater offerings, art exhibits, sporting events, and other special events.
- The **Redwood Empire Association Visitor Information Center** (The Cannery, 2801 Leavenworth St., 2nd Floor, 94133, ☎ 415/543 8334) covers San Francisco and surounding areas, including the Wine Country, the redwood groves, and northwestern California. For $3 they will send *The Redwood Empire Visitor's Guide*; or pick it up at their office for free.
- Chambers of commerce in San Francisco Bay Area towns include **Berkeley** (1834 University Ave., Box 210, Berkeley 94703, ☎ 510/549 7040), and convention and visitors bureaus in **Oakland** (1000 Broadway, Suite 200, Oakland 94607, ☎ 510/839 9000 or 800/262 5526), **San Jose** (333 W. San Carlos St., Suite 1000, San Jose 95110, ☎ 408/295 9600 or 800/726 5673), and **Santa Clara** (2200 Laurelwood Rd., Santa Clara 95054, ☎ 408/970 9825).
- The **California Office of Tourism** (801K St., Suite 1600, Sacramento 95814, ☎ 916/322 1397) can answer questions about travel in the state. You can order a travel package including the *Golden California* guidebook and state map (free; ☎ 800/862 2543).

INDEX

ACKNOWLEDGMENTS

The Automobile Association would like to thank the following photographers, libraries and associations for their assistance in the preparation of this book.

The Automobile Association wishes to thank the following libraries, photographers and associations for their assistance in the preparation of this book
CARTOON ART MUSEUM 53
REX FEATURES LTD 9

All remaining pictures are held in the Association's own library (AA PHOTO LIBRARY) with contributions from H Harris 38b; R Holmes 5a, 5b, 6, 12, 13a, 16, 17, 18, 19, 20, 21, 23b, 24, 25a, 25b, 26b, 28b, 29, 30, 31a, 31b, 32, 33, 34, 35a, 35b, 36a, 36b, 37, 38a, 39, 40a, 40b, 41, 42, 43, 45a, 46, 47a, 48a, 48b, 49b, 50, 52, 54, 55, 56, 57, 58, 59, 60, 87a, 87b; B Smith 7, 27, 49a, 51

Copy-editor: *Beth Ingpen*
Verifier: *Caroline Alder*
Indexer: *Marie Lorimer*
Original design: *Design FX*